RECIPES FROM THE RANCH

Delicious recipes for hearty, home-cooked meals

Publications International, Ltd.

Louis Weber, CEO
Publications International, Ltd.
8140 Lehigh Ave
Morton Grove, IL 60053

Pictured on the front cover: Roasted Chicken & Vegetables *(page 110)*.

Pictured on the back cover *(top to bottom):* Apple-Pear Praline Pie *(page 182),* BBQ Baby Back Ribs *(page 100)* and Bacon & Blue Cheese Chopped Salad *(page 48).*

ISBN: 978-1-63938-140-1

Manufactured in China.

8 7 6 5 4 3 2 1

Microwave Cooking: Microwave ovens vary in wattage. Use the cooking times as guidelines and check for doneness before adding more time.

WARNING: Food preparation, baking and cooking involve inherent dangers: misuse of electric products, sharp electric tools, boiling water, hot stoves, allergic reactions, foodborne illnesses and the like, pose numerous potential risks. Publications International, Ltd. (PIL) assumes no responsibility or liability for any damages you may experience as a result of following recipes, instructions, tips or advice in this publication.

While we hope this publication helps you find new ways to eat delicious foods, you may not always achieve the results desired due to variations in ingredients, cooking temperatures, typos, errors, omissions or individual cooking abilities.

CONTENTS

Smokehouse Barbecued Brisket, *page 44*

BREAKFAST AND BREADS

PUMPKIN CINNAMON ROLLS

Makes 12 rolls

DOUGH

- ½ cup milk
- ¼ cup (½ stick) butter, cut into pieces
- 1 package (¼ ounce) rapid-rise or instant yeast
- ⅔ cup canned pumpkin
- ½ cup packed brown sugar
- 1 egg
- 1 teaspoon salt
- ½ teaspoon pumpkin pie spice
- 3½ to 4 cups all-purpose flour

FILLING

- ¾ cup packed brown sugar
- 2 teaspoons ground cinnamon
- Pinch salt
- ¼ cup (½ stick) butter, softened

GLAZE

- 1 cup powdered sugar
- 2 ounces cream cheese, softened
- 1 to 2 tablespoons milk
- ½ teaspoon vanilla

1. Heat milk and ¼ cup butter in small saucepan over medium heat to 120°F (butter does not need to melt completely). Pour into small bowl. Stir in yeast; let stand 5 minutes or until mixture is bubbly.

2. Combine pumpkin, ½ cup brown sugar, egg, 1 teaspoon salt, pumpkin pie spice and milk mixture in large bowl of stand mixer; beat at low speed until well blended. Add 3½ cups flour; knead with dough hook at low speed 5 to 7 minutes or until dough is smooth and elastic, adding additional flour by tablespoonfuls if necessary.

3. Shape dough into a ball. Place in large greased bowl; turn to grease top. Cover and let rise in warm place 1 hour and 15 minutes or until doubled in size.

4. Spray 13×9-inch baking pan with nonstick cooking spray. For filling, combine ¾ cup brown sugar, cinnamon and pinch of salt in small bowl; mix well. Punch down dough; roll out into 18×14-inch rectangle on lightly floured surface. Spread ¼ cup softened butter over dough; sprinkle with brown sugar mixture. Starting with long end, roll up dough tightly; pinch seam to seal. Trim ends; cut roll crosswise into 12 slices. Place slices cut sides up in prepared pan. Cover and let rise in warm place 45 minutes or until almost doubled. Preheat oven to 350°F.

5. Bake about 20 minutes or until lightly browned. Meanwhile for glaze, whisk powdered sugar, cream cheese, 1 tablespoon milk and vanilla in medium bowl until smooth. Add remaining 1 tablespoon milk to thin glaze, if desired. Drizzle over warm rolls.

BREAKFAST MIGAS

Makes 6 servings

- 1 small ripe avocado, diced
- 1 tablespoon lime juice
- 1 tablespoon olive oil
- 1 small onion, chopped
- 1 jalapeño pepper, seeded and diced
- 3 corn tortillas, torn into 1-inch pieces
- 1 medium tomato, seeded and diced
- 6 eggs
- 2 tablespoons chunky salsa
- Salt and black pepper
- 1 cup (4 ounces) shredded Monterey Jack cheese

1. Combine avocado and lime juice in small bowl; set aside.
2. Heat oil in large nonstick skillet over medium heat. Add onion and jalapeño; cook and stir 5 minutes or until softened.
3. Add tortillas and tomato; cook about 2 minutes or until tomatoes are soft and heated through.
4. Whisk eggs and salsa in medium bowl; season with salt and black pepper. Pour mixture into skillet; cook until eggs are firmly scrambled, stirring occasionally.
5. Remove skillet from heat; stir in cheese. Top each serving with avocado mixture.

LEMON BLUEBERRY OATMEAL

Makes 4 servings

2 tablespoons butter

1¼ cups steel-cut oats

3¾ cups water

½ teaspoon salt

2 lemons

4 tablespoons honey, divided

¾ cup fresh blueberries

½ cup chopped toasted almonds*

To toast almonds, cook in small skillet over medium heat about 5 minutes or until lightly browned and fragrant, stirring frequently.

1. Melt butter in medium saucepan over medium heat. Add oats; cook about 6 minutes or until oats are browned and fragrant, stirring frequently. Stir in water and salt; mix well.
2. Bring to a boil over medium-high heat. Reduce heat to medium-low; cook 20 to 25 minutes or until oats are tender, stirring occasionally.
3. Meanwhile, grate 4 teaspoons peel from lemons; squeeze 3 tablespoons juice.
4. Add lemon juice, 2 teaspoons grated peel and 2 tablespoons honey to oats; mix well. Top each serving with blueberries, almonds and remaining lemon peel; drizzle with remaining honey.

CINNAMON SWIRL COFFEECAKE

Makes 9 to 12 servings

FILLING AND TOPPING

- ⅓ **cup all-purpose flour**
- ⅓ **cup granulated sugar**
- ⅓ **cup packed brown sugar**
- 1½ **tablespoons ground cinnamon**
- ¼ **teaspoon salt**
- ⅛ **teaspoon ground allspice**
- 3 **tablespoons melted butter**

CAKE

- 2 **cups all-purpose flour**
- 1½ **teaspoons baking powder**
- ¾ **teaspoon baking soda**
- ½ **teaspoon salt**
- 9 **tablespoons butter, softened**
- 1¼ **cups granulated sugar**
- 3 **eggs**
- ½ **cup sour cream**
- 2 **teaspoons vanilla**
- ¾ **cup milk**

1. Preheat oven to 350°F. Spray 9-inch square baking pan with nonstick cooking spray.
2. For filling, combine ⅓ cup flour, ⅓ cup granulated sugar, brown sugar, cinnamon, ¼ teaspoon salt and allspice in small bowl; mix well. For topping, remove half of mixture to another small bowl; stir in melted butter until blended.
3. For cake, combine 2 cups flour, baking powder, baking soda and ½ teaspoon salt in medium bowl; mix well.
4. Beat 9 tablespoons butter and 1¼ cups granulated sugar in large bowl with electric mixer at medium speed 3 minutes or until light and fluffy. Add eggs, sour cream and vanilla; beat until well blended. Scrape down side of bowl. Add flour mixture alternately with milk in two additions, beating at low speed until blended. Spread half of batter in prepared pan; sprinkle evenly with filling. Spread remaining batter over filling with dampened hands. Sprinkle with topping.
5. Bake 45 to 50 minutes or until toothpick inserted into center comes out clean. Cool completely in pan on wire rack.

HAM & CHEESE BREAD PUDDING

Makes 8 servings

- 1 small loaf (8 ounces) sourdough, country French or Italian bread, sliced
- 3 tablespoons butter, softened
- 8 ounces ham or smoked ham, cubed
- 1 cup (4 ounces) shredded Cheddar cheese
- 3 eggs
- 2 cups milk
- 1 teaspoon ground mustard
- ½ teaspoon salt
- ⅛ teaspoon white pepper

1. Spray 11×7-inch baking dish with nonstick cooking spray. Spread one side of each bread slice with butter. Cut into 1-inch cubes; spread in prepared baking dish. Top with ham; sprinkle with cheese.

2. Beat eggs in medium bowl. Whisk in milk, mustard, salt and pepper until blended. Pour egg mixture evenly over bread mixture; cover and refrigerate at least 6 hours or overnight.

3. Preheat oven to 350°F. Bake bread pudding, uncovered, 45 to 50 minutes or until puffed and golden brown and knife inserted into center comes out clean. Serve immediately.

GOLDEN CORN BREAD

Makes 9 to 12 servings

- **1¼ cups all-purpose flour**
- **¾ cup yellow cornmeal**
- **⅓ cup sugar**
- **2 teaspoons baking powder**
- **1 teaspoon salt**
- **1¼ cups whole milk**
- **¼ cup (½ stick) butter, melted**
- **1 egg**
- **Honey Butter (recipe follows, optional)**

1. Preheat oven to 400°F. Spray 8-inch square baking dish or pan with nonstick cooking spray.
2. Combine flour, cornmeal, sugar, baking powder and salt in large bowl; mix well. Whisk milk, butter and egg in medium bowl until well blended. Add to flour mixture; stir just until dry ingredients are moistened. Pour batter into prepared baking dish.
3. Bake 25 minutes or until golden brown and toothpick inserted into center comes out clean. Prepare Honey Butter, if desired; serve with corn bread.

Honey Butter: Beat 6 tablespoons (¾ stick) softened butter and ¼ cup honey in medium bowl with electric mixer at medium-high speed until light and creamy.

STUFFED TOMATOES & CREAMED SPINACH

Makes 4 servings

- 4 medium tomatoes
- ¼ cup plus 1 tablespoon grated Parmesan cheese, divided
- 4 eggs
- 4 teaspoons minced green onion
- Salt and black pepper
- 2 tablespoons butter
- 2 tablespoons all-purpose flour
- 1 cup milk
- 1 package (10 ounces) frozen chopped spinach, thawed and squeezed dry

1. Preheat oven to 375°F.
2. Cut thin slice off stem end of each tomato; remove seeds and pulp, being careful not to pierce side of tomato. Place tomato shells in shallow baking dish.
3. Sprinkle 1 tablespoon cheese inside each tomato. Break an egg into each tomato. Top with onion, salt and pepper. Bake 15 to 20 minutes or until eggs are set.
4. Meanwhile for creamed spinach, melt butter in medium saucepan over medium heat. Stir in flour; cook until bubbly. Gradually stir in milk; cook and stir until thickened. Reduce heat to low; stir in spinach. Cook about 5 minutes or until spinach is tender and heated through, stirring occasionally. Stir in remaining 1 tablespoon cheese; season to taste with salt and pepper. Serve with tomatoes.

QUICK CASSEROLE BREAD

Makes 1 loaf

- **2¾ cups all-purpose flour**
- **3 tablespoons nonfat dry milk powder**
- **1 package (¼ ounce) rapid-rise or instant yeast**
- **2 tablespoons sugar**
- **1 teaspoon salt**
- **1 cup warm water (120°F)**
- **2 tablespoons vegetable oil**
- **1 tablespoon sesame or poppy seeds (optional)**

1. Combine flour, milk powder, yeast, sugar and salt in large bowl of stand mixer fitted with dough hook. Turn mixer to low; mix 1 minute. With mixer running, add water and oil. Knead at low speed 5 minutes.
2. Spray 1½-quart round baking dish with nonstick cooking spray. Scrape batter into prepared baking dish; smooth top and sprinkle with sesame seeds, if desired. Cover and let stand in warm place 45 minutes or until almost doubled.
3. Preheat oven to 375°F. Bake 25 to 30 minutes or until wooden skewer inserted into center comes out clean (190° to 200°F on instant-read thermometer). Cool in baking dish 10 minutes. Remove to wire rack; cool completely.

Casserole Cheese Bread: Prepare batter as directed for Quick Casserole Bread. Pour half of the batter into greased 1½-quart baking dish. Sprinkle 1 cup cubed Cheddar or Swiss cheese over batter. Pour remaining batter over cheese. Stir gently to mix in cheese. Let rise and bake as directed above.

Honey Wheat Casserole Bread: Prepare batter as directed for Quick Casserole Bread using 1½ cups all-purpose flour and 1 cup whole wheat flour, and substituting honey for sugar. Let rise and bake as directed above.

Oatmeal Casserole Bread: Prepare batter as directed for Quick Casserole Bread using 1¾ cups flour and 1 cup uncooked quick or old-fashioned oats. Let rise and bake as directed above. Sprinkle with additional oats before baking, if desired.

RHUBARB BREAD

Makes 1 loaf (about 12 servings)

- 2 cups all-purpose flour
- 1 cup sugar
- 1 tablespoon baking powder
- 1 teaspoon salt
- ¼ teaspoon ground cinnamon
- 1 cup milk
- 2 eggs
- ⅓ cup butter, melted
- 2 teaspoons grated fresh ginger (about 1 inch)
- 10 ounces chopped fresh rhubarb (¼-inch pieces, about 2¼ cups total)
- ¾ cup chopped walnuts, toasted*

**To toast walnuts, spread on ungreased baking sheet. Bake in preheated 350°F oven 6 to 8 minutes or until lightly browned, stirring frequently.*

1. Preheat oven to 350°F. Spray 9×5-inch loaf pan with nonstick cooking spray.
2. Combine flour, sugar, baking powder, salt and cinnamon in large bowl; mix well. Whisk milk, eggs, butter and ginger in medium bowl until well blended. Add to flour mixture; stir just until dry ingredients are moistened. Add rhubarb and walnuts; stir just until blended. Pour batter into prepared pan.
3. Bake about 1 hour or until toothpick inserted into center comes out clean. Cool in pan on wire rack 15 minutes. Remove to wire rack; cool completely.

STUFFED HASH BROWNS

Makes 1 to 2 servings

- 1½ cups shredded potatoes*
- 2 tablespoons finely chopped onion
- ¼ plus ⅛ teaspoon salt, divided
- ⅛ teaspoon black pepper
- 2 tablespoons butter, divided
- 1 tablespoon vegetable oil
- ½ cup diced ham (¼-inch pieces)
- 3 eggs
- 2 tablespoons milk
- 2 slices American cheese

****Use refrigerated shredded hash brown potatoes or shredded peeled russet potatoes, squeezed dry.***

1. Preheat oven to 250°F. Place wire rack over baking sheet. Combine potatoes, onion, ¼ teaspoon salt and pepper in medium bowl; mix well.
2. Heat 1 tablespoon butter and oil in small (6- to 8-inch) nonstick skillet over medium heat. Add potato mixture; spread to cover bottom of skillet evenly, pressing down gently with spatula to flatten. Cook about 10 minutes or until bottom and edges are golden brown. Cover skillet with large inverted plate; carefully flip hash browns onto plate. Slide hash browns back into skillet, cooked side up. Cook 10 minutes or until golden brown. Slide hash browns onto prepared wire rack; place in oven to keep warm while preparing ham and eggs.
3. Melt 1 teaspoon butter in same skillet over medium-high heat. Add ham; cook and stir 2 to 3 minutes or until lightly browned. Remove to plate.
4. Whisk eggs, milk and remaining ⅛ teaspoon salt in small bowl. Melt remaining 2 teaspoons butter in same skillet over medium-high heat. Add egg mixture; cook about 3 minutes or just until eggs are cooked through, stirring to form large, fluffy curds. Place cheese slices on top of eggs; remove from heat and cover skillet with lid or foil to melt cheese.
5. Cut hash browns in half. Place one half on serving plate; sprinkle with ham. Top with eggs and remaining half of hash browns.

Tip: Refrigerated shredded potatoes are very wet when removed from the package. For the best results, dry them well with paper towels before cooking.

SANDWICHES AND BURGERS

BARBECUE BEEF SANDWICHES

Makes 4 servings

- **2½ pounds boneless beef chuck roast**
- **2 tablespoons Southwest seasoning**
- **1 tablespoon vegetable oil**
- **1¼ cups beef broth**
- **2½ cups barbecue sauce, divided**
- **4 sandwich or pretzel buns, split**
- **1⅓ cups prepared coleslaw* (preferably vinegar based)**

**Vinegar-based coleslaws provide a perfect complement to the rich beef; they can often be found at the salad bar, deli counter or prepared foods section of large supermarkets.*

1. Sprinkle both sides of beef with Southwest seasoning. Heat oil in Dutch oven over medium-high heat. Add beef; cook about 6 minutes per side or until browned. Remove to plate.
2. Add broth; cook 2 minutes, scraping up browned bits from bottom of Dutch oven. Stir in 2 cups barbecue sauce; bring to a boil. Return beef to Dutch oven; turn to coat.
3. Reduce heat to low; cover and cook 3 to 3½ hours or until beef is fork-tender, turning beef halfway through cooking time.
4. Remove beef to large bowl; let stand until cool enough to handle. Meanwhile, cook sauce remaining in Dutch oven over high heat about 10 minutes or until reduced and slightly thickened.
5. Shred beef into bite-size pieces. Stir in 1 cup reduced cooking sauce and ¼ cup barbecue sauce. Taste and add remaining ¼ cup barbecue sauce, if desired. Fill buns with beef mixture; top with coleslaw.

CRISPY CHICKEN SANDWICHES

Makes 4 servings

- 2 boneless skinless chicken breasts (6 to 8 ounces each)
- 4 cups cold water
- ¼ cup granulated sugar
- 3 tablespoons plus 1 teaspoon salt, divided
- Peanut or vegetable oil for frying
- 1 cup milk
- 2 eggs
- 1½ cups all-purpose flour
- 2 tablespoons powdered sugar
- 2 teaspoons paprika
- 2 teaspoons black pepper
- ¾ teaspoon baking powder
- ½ teaspoon ground red pepper
- 8 dill pickle slices
- 4 soft hamburger buns, toasted and buttered

1. Pound chicken to ½-inch thickness between two sheets of waxed paper or plastic wrap with rolling pin or meat mallet. Cut each breast in half crosswise to create total of four pieces.
2. Combine water, granulated sugar and 3 tablespoons salt in medium bowl; stir until sugar and salt are dissolved. Add chicken to brine; cover and refrigerate 2 to 4 hours. Remove chicken from refrigerator about 30 minutes before cooking.
3. Heat 3 inches of oil in large saucepan over medium-high heat to 350°F; adjust heat to maintain temperature during cooking. Meanwhile, beat milk and eggs in shallow bowl until blended. Combine flour, powdered sugar, paprika, black pepper, remaining 1 teaspoon salt, baking powder and red pepper in another shallow bowl; mix well.
4. Working with one piece at a time, remove chicken from brine and add to milk mixture, turning to coat. Place in flour mixture; turn to coat completely and shake off excess. Lower chicken gently into hot oil; fry 6 to 8 minutes or until cooked through (165°F) and crust is golden brown and crisp, turning occasionally. Drain on paper towel-lined plate.
5. Place two pickle slices on bottom halves of buns; top with chicken and top halves of buns. Serve immediately.

BLT SUPREME

Makes 2 servings

- **12 to 16 slices thick-cut bacon**
- **⅓ cup mayonnaise**
- **1½ teaspoons minced chipotle pepper in adobo sauce**
- **1 teaspoon lime juice**
- **1 ripe avocado**
- **⅛ teaspoon salt**
- **⅛ teaspoon black pepper**
- **4 leaves romaine lettuce**
- **½ baguette, cut into 2 (8-inch) lengths *or* 2 hoagie rolls, split and toasted**
- **6 to 8 slices tomato**

1. Cook bacon in large skillet over medium heat or on baking sheet in oven until crisp-chewy. Drain on paper towel-lined plate.
2. Meanwhile, combine mayonnaise, chipotle pepper and lime juice in small bowl; mix well. Coarsely mash avocado in another small bowl; stir in salt and black pepper. Cut romaine leaves crosswise into ¼-inch strips.
3. For each sandwich, spread heaping tablespoon of mayonnaise mixture on bottom half of baguette; top with one fourth of lettuce. Arrange 3 to 4 slices bacon over lettuce; spread 2 tablespoons mashed avocado over bacon. Drizzle with heaping tablespoon of mayonnaise mixture. Top with 3 to 4 tomato slices, one fourth of lettuce and 3 to 4 slices bacon. Close sandwich with top half of baguette.

HEARTY VEGGIE SANDWICHES

Makes 4 servings

- **1 pound cremini mushrooms, stemmed and thinly sliced (⅛-inch slices)**
- **2 tablespoons olive oil, divided**
- **¾ teaspoon salt, divided**
- **¼ teaspoon black pepper**
- **1 medium zucchini, diced (¼-inch pieces, about 2 cups)**
- **3 tablespoons butter, softened**
- **8 slices artisan whole grain bread**
- **¼ cup pesto sauce**
- **¼ cup mayonnaise**
- **2 cups packed baby spinach**
- **4 slices mozzarella cheese**

1. Preheat oven to 350°F. Combine mushrooms, 1 tablespoon oil, ½ teaspoon salt and pepper in medium bowl; toss to coat. Spread in single layer on large baking sheet. Roast 20 minutes or until mushrooms are dark brown and dry, stirring after 10 minutes. Cool on baking sheet.

2. Meanwhile, heat remaining 1 tablespoon oil in large skillet over medium heat. Add zucchini and remaining ¼ teaspoon salt; cook and stir 5 minutes or until zucchini is tender and lightly browned. Remove to medium bowl; wipe out skillet with paper towels.

3. Spread butter on one side of each bread slice. Turn over slices. Spread pesto on four bread slices; spread mayonnaise on remaining four slices. Top pesto-covered slices evenly with mushrooms; layer with spinach, zucchini and cheese. Top with remaining bread slices, mayonnaise side down.

4. Heat same skillet over medium heat. Add sandwiches; cover and cook 2 minutes per side or until bread is toasted, spinach is slightly wilted and cheese is beginning to melt. Serve immediately.

DELUXE BACON & GOUDA BURGERS

Makes 4 servings

- ⅓ cup mayonnaise
- 1 teaspoon minced garlic
- ¼ teaspoon Dijon mustard
- 1½ pounds ground beef
- Salt and black pepper
- 2 thick slices red onion
- 4 to 8 slices Gouda cheese
- Butter lettuce leaves
- 4 onion rolls, split and toasted
- Tomato slices
- 4 to 8 slices bacon, crisp-cooked

1. Combine mayonnaise, garlic and mustard in small bowl; refrigerate until ready to serve.

2. Prepare grill for direct cooking. Shape beef into four patties, about ¾ inch thick; season both sides with salt and pepper.

3. Grill patties and onion over medium-high heat, covered, 8 to 10 minutes (or uncovered, 13 to 15 minutes) to medium (160°F) or to desired doneness, turning once. Remove onion when browned and softened. Top with cheese during last 2 minutes of grilling.

4. Separate onion into rings. Place lettuce on bottom half of each roll; top with mayonnaise mixture, burger, tomato, onion rings, bacon and top half of roll.

TURKEY ONION DIP

Makes 6 servings

HERB-ROASTED TURKEY

- 1 small bone-in turkey breast (4 to 5 pounds)
- 1½ tablespoons olive oil
- 2 cloves garlic, minced
- 2 teaspoons coarse salt
- 1 teaspoon dried rosemary
- 1 teaspoon dried sage
- ½ teaspoon dried thyme
- ½ teaspoon black pepper

SANDWICHES

- 1 tablespoon olive oil
- 2 large onions, cut in half crosswise then cut vertically into ¼-inch slices (about 2 cups)
- ¼ cup water
- ½ teaspoon salt, plus additional for seasoning
- 1½ cups sour cream
- ⅓ cup prepared horseradish
- 3 tablespoons Dijon mustard
- Black pepper
- 6 hoagie or sub rolls, split and toasted
- 12 slices Swiss cheese (about 1 ounce each)

1. For turkey, preheat oven to 400°F. Place turkey breast on rack in small roasting or baking pan. Pat skin dry with paper towel.
2. Combine 1½ tablespoons oil, garlic, 2 teaspoons salt, rosemary, sage, thyme and ½ teaspoon pepper in small bowl; mix well. Rub mixture all over turkey breast. (If desired, loosen skin and rub some of oil mixture directly on turkey meat.) Place turkey in oven; *reduce oven temperature to 350°F.* Roast 1 hour and 15 minutes or until cooked through (165°F). Let rest 15 minutes.
3. Meanwhile for sandwiches, heat 1 tablespoon oil in large skillet over medium-high heat. Add onions; cook 20 minutes or until onions begin to brown, stirring occasionally. Add water and ½ teaspoon salt. Reduce heat to medium; cook 20 minutes or until golden brown, stirring occasionally.
4. Combine sour cream, horseradish and mustard in medium bowl; stir until well blended. Refrigerate until ready to assemble sandwiches.
5. Shred turkey into bite-size pieces; place in large bowl. Drizzle with pan juices and season with salt and pepper; toss to coat.
6. Spread cut sides of each roll with about 1½ tablespoons sour cream mixture. Top bottom halves of rolls with 2 cups turkey, caramelized onions, 2 slices cheese and top halves of rolls. Serve warm.

BACKYARD BARBECUE BURGERS

Makes 6 servings

- 1½ pounds ground beef
- 5 tablespoons barbecue sauce, divided
- Salt and black pepper
- 1 onion, cut into thick slices
- 1 tomato, sliced
- 2 tablespoons olive oil
- 6 Kaiser rolls, split
- 6 leaves green or red leaf lettuce

1. Prepare grill for direct cooking. Combine beef and 2 tablespoons barbecue sauce in large bowl. Shape into six 1-inch-thick patties; season both sides with salt and pepper.
2. Grill patties, covered, over medium heat 8 to 10 minutes (or uncovered 13 to 15 minutes) to medium (160°F) or to desired doneness, turning once. Brush both sides with remaining 3 tablespoons barbecue sauce during last 5 minutes of cooking.
3. Meanwhile, brush onion and tomato slices with oil. Grill onion slices about 10 minutes and tomato slices 2 to 3 minutes.
4. Just before serving, place rolls, cut side down, on grid; grill until lightly toasted. Serve burgers on rolls with tomato, onion and lettuce.

HONEY-MUSTARD & BEER PULLED PORK SANDWICHES

Makes 8 servings

- 1 tablespoon chili powder
- 2 teaspoons ground cumin
- ½ teaspoon salt
- 2 tablespoons yellow mustard
- 2 pounds bone-in pork shoulder roast
- 2 bottles (12 ounces each) beer, divided
- ¾ cup ketchup
- 3 tablespoons honey
- 2 tablespoons cider vinegar
- 8 soft sandwich rolls
- 24 bread and butter pickle chips

1. Prepare grill for indirect cooking over medium-low heat.
2. Combine chili powder, cumin and salt in small bowl. Spread mustard on all sides of pork, then cover evenly with cumin mixture. Transfer pork to rack in disposable foil pan. Reserve ¾ cup beer. Pour enough remaining beer into foil pan to just cover rack beneath pork. Place tray on grid opposite heat source.
3. Grill, covered, 4 to 6 hours or until internal temperature reaches 160°F. Transfer to cutting board; tent with foil and let stand 15 minutes.
4. Combine reserved ¾ cup beer, ketchup, honey and vinegar in small saucepan. Bring to a boil over medium-high heat. Reduce heat to medium; cook and stir until thickened.
5. Shred pork with two forks, discarding any bone, fat or connective tissue. Combine pork and sauce in medium bowl; toss gently to combine. Serve on rolls with pickles.

SMOKEHOUSE BARBECUED BRISKET

Makes 6 servings

- 1 beef brisket, trimmed (about 3 to 4 pounds)
- Salt and black pepper
- 1 tablespoon garlic powder
- 3 tablespoons olive oil
- 1 onion, minced
- 1 cup beef broth
- 1 tablespoon liquid smoke
- ½ teaspoon red pepper flakes
- ½ cup plus 1 can (12 ounces) cola beverage, divided
- 4 tablespoons packed dark brown sugar, divided
- 2 cups tomato sauce
- 2 tablespoons onion powder
- 2 tablespoons hot pepper sauce
- 1 tablespoon Worcestershire sauce
- Kaiser rolls or hamburger buns

1. Preheat oven to 250°F. Season brisket generously with salt, black pepper and garlic powder. Heat oil in Dutch oven over medium-high heat. Add brisket; cook 4 to 5 minutes per side or until browned. Remove brisket to plate.

2. Add onion to Dutch oven; cook and stir 5 minutes or until softened. Add broth, liquid smoke and red pepper flakes, stirring to scrape up browned bits. Return brisket to Dutch oven; pour in ½ cup cola and sprinkle 2 tablespoons brown sugar over brisket.

3. Bake 5 to 6 hours or until meat is falling apart, basting every 30 minutes. Remove brisket to cutting board; set aside.

4. *Increase heat to 400°F.* Stir remaining 2 tablespoons brown sugar, tomato sauce, remaining 1 can of cola, onion powder, hot pepper sauce and Worcestershire sauce into liquid in Dutch oven. Bake 30 minutes.

5. When brisket is cool enough to handle, cut into ½-inch slices. Return brisket to Dutch oven and baste with sauce. *Reduce heat to 250°F.* Bake 30 minutes. Serve brisket slices on rolls.

SOUPS AND SALADS

BACON & BLUE CHEESE CHOPPED SALAD

Makes 8 to 10 servings (20 cups)

DRESSING

- ⅓ cup white balsamic vinegar
- ¼ cup Dijon mustard
- 1 package (about 2 tablespoons) Italian salad dressing mix
- ⅔ cup extra virgin olive oil

SALAD

- 1 medium head iceberg lettuce, chopped
- 1 medium head romaine lettuce, chopped
- 1 can (about 14 ounces) hearts of palm or artichoke hearts, quartered lengthwise then sliced crosswise
- 1 large avocado, diced
- 1½ cups crumbled blue cheese
- 2 hard-cooked eggs, chopped
- 1 ripe tomato, chopped
- ½ small red onion, finely chopped
- 12 slices bacon, crisp-cooked and crumbled

1. For dressing, whisk vinegar, mustard and dressing mix in small bowl. Gradually whisk in oil in thin, steady stream. Set aside until ready to use. (Dressing can be made up to 1 week in advance; refrigerate in jar with tight-fitting lid.)
2. For salad, combine lettuce, hearts of palm, avocado, cheese, eggs, tomato, onion and bacon in large bowl. Add dressing; toss to coat.

CLASSIC CHILI

Makes 6 servings

- **1½ pounds ground beef**
- **1½ cups chopped onion**
- **1 cup chopped green bell pepper**
- **2 cloves garlic, minced**
- **3 cans (about 15 ounces each) dark red kidney beans, rinsed and drained**
- **2 cans (about 15 ounces each) tomato sauce**
- **1 can (about 14 ounces) diced tomatoes**
- **2 to 3 teaspoons chili powder**
- **1 to 2 teaspoons dry mustard**
- **¾ teaspoon dried basil**
- **½ teaspoon black pepper**
- **1 to 2 dried hot chile peppers (optional)**
- **Shredded Cheddar cheese (optional)**

SLOW COOKER DIRECTIONS

1. Heat large skillet over medium-high heat. Add beef, onion, bell pepper and garlic; cook 6 to 8 minutes or until beef is browned and onion is softened, stirring to break up meat. Drain fat. Transfer to slow cooker.
2. Add beans, tomato sauce, diced tomatoes, chili powder, dry mustard, basil, black pepper and chile peppers, if desired, to slow cooker; mix well.
3. Cover; cook on LOW 8 to 10 hours or on HIGH 4 to 5 hours. Remove and discard chile peppers before serving. Top with cheese, if desired.

AUTUMN HARVEST SALAD

Makes 6 servings

DRESSING

- ½ cup extra virgin olive oil
- 3 tablespoons balsamic vinegar
- 1 clove garlic, minced
- 1 teaspoon honey
- 1 teaspoon Dijon mustard
- ½ teaspoon dried oregano
- ½ teaspoon salt
- ⅛ teaspoon black pepper

SALAD

- 1 loaf (12 to 16 ounces) artisan pecan raisin bread
- ¼ cup (½ stick) butter, melted
- 6 tablespoons coarse sugar (such as demerara or turbinado sugar)
- 6 cups packed spring greens
- 2 Granny Smith apples, thinly sliced
- 18 to 24 ounces grilled chicken breast strips
- ¾ cup crumbled blue cheese
- ¾ cup dried cranberries
- ¾ cup toasted walnuts*

**To toast walnuts, cook in small skillet over medium heat about 5 minutes or until lightly browned and fragrant, stirring frequently.*

1. For dressing, whisk oil, vinegar, garlic, honey, mustard, oregano, salt and pepper in medium bowl until well blended. Refrigerate until ready to use.

2. Preheat oven to 350°F. Line baking sheet with parchment paper. Cut bread into thin (¼-inch) slices; place in single layer on prepared baking sheet. Brush one side of each slice with melted butter; sprinkle each slice with ½ teaspoon sugar. Bake 10 minutes. Turn slices; brush with butter and sprinkle with ½ teaspoon sugar. Bake 10 minutes. Cool completely on baking sheet.

3. For each salad, place 1 cup greens on serving plate. Top with ½ cup apple slices, ¼ cup chicken strips and 2 tablespoons each cheese, cranberries and walnuts. Break 2 toast slices into pieces and sprinkle over salad. Drizzle with 2 tablespoons dressing.

SALSA VERDE CHICKEN STEW

Makes 4 to 6 servings

- 1 tablespoon vegetable oil
- 1½ pounds boneless skinless chicken breasts, cut into ¾-inch pieces
- 2 cans (about 15 ounces each) black beans, rinsed and drained
- 1 jar (24 ounces) salsa verde
- 1½ cups frozen corn
- ¾ cup chopped fresh cilantro
- Optional toppings: diced avocado, sour cream and/or tortilla chips

1. Heat oil in large saucepan over medium-high heat. Add chicken; cook and stir 5 minutes or until chicken begins to brown.
2. Stir in beans and salsa; bring to a simmer. Reduce heat to low; cover and cook 8 minutes.
3. Stir in corn; cook, uncovered, 3 minutes or until heated through. Remove from heat; stir in cilantro. Serve with desired toppings.

BROCCOLI & CAULIFLOWER SALAD

Makes 8 servings

- **1 package (about 12 ounces) bacon, chopped**
- **2 cups mayonnaise**
- **¼ cup sugar**
- **¼ cup white or apple cider vinegar**
- **4 cups chopped raw broccoli**
- **4 cups coarsely chopped raw cauliflower**
- **1½ cups (6 ounces) shredded Cheddar cheese**
- **1 cup chopped red onion**
- **1 cup dried cranberries or raisins (optional)**
- **½ cup sunflower seeds (optional)**
- **Salt and black pepper**

1. Cook bacon in large skillet over medium heat until crisp, stirring occasionally. Remove from skillet with slotted spoon; drain on paper towel-lined plate.
2. Whisk mayonnaise, sugar and vinegar in large bowl. Stir in broccoli, cauliflower, cheese, onion and cranberries, if desired; mix well. Fold in bacon and sunflower seeds, if desired. Season with salt and pepper.
3. Serve immediately or cover and refrigerate until ready to serve.

BEEF VEGETABLE SOUP

Makes 6 to 8 servings (about 12 cups)

- 1½ pounds cubed beef stew meat
- ¼ cup all-purpose flour
- 3 tablespoons vegetable oil, divided
- 1 onion, chopped
- 2 stalks celery, chopped
- 3 tablespoons tomato paste
- 2 teaspoons salt
- 1 teaspoon dried thyme
- ½ teaspoon garlic powder
- ¼ teaspoon black pepper
- 6 cups beef broth, divided
- 1 can (28 ounces) stewed tomatoes, undrained
- 1 tablespoon Worcestershire sauce
- 1 bay leaf
- 4 unpeeled red potatoes (about 1 pound), cut into 1-inch pieces
- 3 medium carrots, cut in half lengthwise and cut into ½-inch slices
- 6 ounces green beans, trimmed and cut into 1-inch pieces
- 1 cup frozen corn

1. Combine beef and flour in medium bowl; toss to coat. Heat 1 tablespoon oil in large saucepan or Dutch oven over medium-high heat. Cook beef in two batches 5 minutes or until browned, adding additional 1 tablespoon oil after first batch. Remove beef to medium bowl.

2. Heat remaining 1 tablespoon oil in same saucepan. Add onion and celery; cook and stir 5 minutes or until softened. Add tomato paste, salt, thyme, garlic powder and pepper; cook and stir 1 minute. Stir in 1 cup broth, scraping up browned bits from bottom of saucepan. Stir in remaining 5 cups broth, tomatoes with juice, Worcestershire sauce, bay leaf and beef; bring to a boil.

3. Reduce heat to low; cover and simmer 1 hour and 20 minutes. Add potatoes and carrots; cook 15 minutes. Add green beans and corn; cook 15 minutes or until vegetables are tender. Remove and discard bay leaf before serving.

GREEN BEAN POTATO SALAD

Makes 6 servings

Pickled Red Onions (recipe follows)

- **2 cups cubed assorted potatoes (purple, baby red and/or Yukon Gold)**
- **1 cup fresh green beans, cut into 1-inch pieces**
- **2 tablespoons plain Greek yogurt or sour cream**
- **2 tablespoons white wine vinegar**
- **2 tablespoons olive oil**
- **1 tablespoon spicy mustard**
- **1 teaspoon salt**

1. Prepare Pickled Red Onions.
2. Bring large saucepan of water to a boil. Add potatoes; cook 5 to 8 minutes or until fork-tender.* Add green beans during last 4 minutes of cooking time. Drain potatoes and green beans.
3. Whisk yogurt, vinegar, oil, mustard and salt in large bowl until smooth and well blended.
4. Add potatoes, green beans and Pickled Red Onions to dressing; toss gently to coat. Cover and refrigerate at least 1 hour before serving to allow flavors to develop.

**Some potatoes may take longer to cook than others. Remove individual potatoes to large bowl using slotted spoon when fork-tender.*

Pickled Red Onions: Combine ½ cup thinly sliced red onion, ¼ cup white wine vinegar, 2 tablespoons water, 1 teaspoon sugar and ½ teaspoon salt in large glass jar. Seal jar; shake well. Refrigerate at least 1 hour or up to 1 week.

FIESTA CORN SALAD

Makes 4 to 6 servings

DRESSING

- 1 cup plain yogurt
- 3 tablespoons minced onion
- 1½ tablespoons fresh lime juice
- 1 clove garlic, minced
- 1 teaspoon ground cumin
- 1 teaspoon chili powder
- ¼ teaspoon salt

SALAD

- 5 large ears fresh corn
- 1½ cups shredded red cabbage
- 1 large tomato, chopped
- 1 medium green bell pepper, seeded and chopped
- 5 slices bacon, cooked and crumbled (optional)
- 1 cup coarsely crushed tortilla chips
- 1 cup (4 ounces) shredded Cheddar cheese

1. For dressing, combine yogurt, onion, lime juice, garlic, cumin, chili powder and salt in small bowl; mix well.
2. Bring large saucepan of water to a boil. Remove husks and silk from corn; place in boiling water. Cover and cook 6 minutes or until tender; drain and cool completely. Cut corn from cob using sharp knife.
3. Combine corn, cabbage, tomato and bell pepper in large bowl. Pour dressing over vegetables; mix well. Cover and refrigerate until ready to serve. Stir in bacon just before serving, if desired. Sprinkle with chips and cheese.

GERMAN FRUIT SALAD

Makes 8 servings

2 jars (16 ounces each) maraschino cherries, drained

2 cans (11 ounces each) mandarin oranges, drained

1 can (20 ounces) fruit cocktail, drained

1 container (16 ounces) sour cream

1 tablespoon mayonnaise

Chopped walnuts (optional)

2 large red apples, cut into bite-size pieces

2 bananas, cut into bite-size pieces

1. Combine cherries, oranges and fruit cocktail in large bowl.
2. Whisk sour cream and mayonnaise in medium bowl; stir into fruit mixture. Add chopped walnuts, if desired; mix well.
3. Cover; refrigerate 2 hours. Add apples and bananas just before serving; mix well.

EASY CORN CHOWDER

Makes 6 servings

- 2 cans (about 14 ounces each) vegetable or chicken broth
- 1 bag (16 ounces) frozen corn, thawed
- 3 small potatoes, peeled and cut into ½-inch pieces
- 1 red bell pepper, diced
- 1 medium onion, diced
- 1 stalk celery, sliced
- ½ teaspoon salt
- ½ teaspoon black pepper
- ¼ teaspoon ground coriander
- ½ cup whipping cream
- 4 slices bacon, crisp-cooked and crumbled (optional)

SLOW COOKER DIRECTIONS

1. Combine broth, corn, potatoes, bell pepper, onion, celery, salt, black pepper and coriander in slow cooker. Cover; cook on LOW 7 to 8 hours.
2. Turn slow cooker to HIGH. Partially mash soup mixture with potato masher to thicken. Stir in cream; cook on HIGH, uncovered, until hot. Adjust seasonings. Top with bacon, if desired.

COLESLAW WITH SNOW PEAS & CORN

Makes 4 servings

- **4 cups (about 8 ounces) coleslaw mix**
- **½ cup trimmed vertically sliced snow peas**
- **½ cup corn (frozen or fresh)**
- **¼ cup mayonnaise**
- **¼ cup sour cream**
- **¼ cup buttermilk**
- **1 tablespoon cider vinegar**
- **2 teaspoons sugar**
- **¼ teaspoon celery seed**
- **Salt and black pepper**

1. Combine coleslaw, snow peas and corn in large bowl.
2. Whisk mayonnaise, sour cream, buttermilk, vinegar, sugar and celery seed in medium bowl. Add to coleslaw mixture; stir until well blended. Season with salt and pepper to taste.

COUNTRY CHICKEN CHOWDER

Makes 4 servings

- 1 pound chicken tenders
- 2 tablespoons butter
- 1 small onion, chopped
- 1 stalk celery, sliced
- 1 small carrot, sliced
- 1 can (10¾ ounces) condensed cream of potato soup, undiluted
- 1 cup milk
- 1 cup frozen corn
- ½ teaspoon dried dill
- Salt and black pepper
- Croutons (optional)

1. Cut chicken tenders into ½-inch pieces.
2. Melt butter in large saucepan or Dutch oven over medium-high heat. Add chicken; cook and stir 5 minutes.
3. Add onion, celery and carrot; cook and stir 3 minutes. Stir in soup, milk, corn and dill; reduce heat to low. Cook about 8 minutes or until corn is tender and chowder is heated through. Season with salt and pepper to taste. Serve with croutons, if desired.

CASSEROLES AND BAKES

CHEESEBURGER POTATO CASSEROLE

Makes 6 servings

- 1 pound ground beef
- ½ cup chopped onion
- 1 can (about 10¾ ounces) Cheddar cheese soup
- ¼ cup sweet pickle relish
- 2 tablespoons brown mustard
- 2 tablespoons ketchup, plus additional for topping
- 1 tablespoon Worcestershire sauce
- 1 package (30 ounces) shredded potatoes
- 2 cups (8 ounces) shredded Cheddar cheese
- 1 teaspoon salt
- ½ teaspoon black pepper
- Sliced green onions (optional)

SLOW COOKER DIRECTIONS

1. Coat inside of slow cooker with nonstick cooking spray. Heat large skillet over medium-high heat. Add beef and onion; cook 6 to 8 minutes or until beef is browned and onion is softened, stirring to break up meat. Drain fat. Stir in soup, relish, mustard, 2 tablespoons ketchup and Worcestershire sauce until well blended.
2. Arrange half of potatoes in bottom of slow cooker. Spoon half of meat mixture over potatoes. Sprinkle with 1½ cups cheese, ½ teaspoon salt and ¼ teaspoon pepper. Top with remaining half of potatoes. Add remaining half of meat mixture; sprinkle with remaining ½ cup cheese, ½ teaspoon salt and ¼ teaspoon pepper.
3. Cover; cook on LOW 4 hours or on HIGH 2 hours. Top with additional ketchup and green onions, if desired.

SAUSAGE & BEAN SKILLET

Makes 4 to 6 servings

- 2 cups fresh bread crumbs*
- 2 tablespoons olive oil, divided
- 1 pound uncooked pork sausage, cut into 2-inch pieces
- 1 leek, white and light green parts only, cut in half and thinly sliced
- 1 large onion, cut into quarters then cut into ¼-inch slices
- 1 teaspoon salt, divided
- 2 cloves garlic, minced
- ½ teaspoon dried thyme
- ½ teaspoon ground sage
- ¼ teaspoon paprika
- ¼ teaspoon ground allspice
- ¼ teaspoon black pepper
- 1 can (28 ounces) diced tomatoes
- 2 cans (about 15 ounces each) navy or cannellini beans, rinsed and drained
- 2 tablespoons whole grain mustard
- Fresh thyme leaves (optional)

***To make bread crumbs, cut 4 ounces of stale baguette or country bread into several pieces; place in food processor. Pulse until coarse crumbs form.**

1. Preheat oven to 350°F. Combine bread crumbs and 1 tablespoon oil in medium bowl; mix well.

2. Heat remaining 1 tablespoon oil in large ovenproof skillet over medium-high heat. Add sausage; cook 8 minutes or until browned, stirring occasionally. (Sausage will not be cooked through.) Remove to plate.

3. Add leek, onion and ½ teaspoon salt to skillet; cook 10 minutes or until vegetables are soft and beginning to brown, stirring occasionally. Add garlic; cook and stir 1 minute. Add dried thyme, sage, paprika, allspice and pepper; cook and stir 1 minute. Add tomatoes; cook 5 minutes, stirring occasionally. Stir in beans, mustard and remaining ½ teaspoon salt; bring to a simmer.

4. Return sausage to skillet, pushing down into bean mixture. Sprinkle with bread crumbs.

5. Bake 25 minutes or until bread crumbs are lightly browned and sausage is cooked through. Garnish with fresh thyme.

CHILE-CORN QUICHE

Makes 6 servings

- **1 can (8¾ ounces) whole kernel corn, drained *or* 1 cup corn, cooked**
- **1 can (4 ounces) diced mild green chiles, drained**
- **¼ cup thinly sliced green onions**
- **1 unbaked frozen 9-inch pie crust**
- **1 cup (4 ounces) shredded Monterey Jack cheese**
- **1½ cups half-and-half**
- **3 eggs**
- **½ teaspoon salt**
- **½ teaspoon ground cumin**

1. Preheat oven to 375°F.
2. Combine corn, chiles and green onions in small bowl. Spoon into crust; top with cheese. Whisk half-and-half, eggs, salt and cumin in medium bowl. Pour over cheese.
3. Bake 40 to 45 minutes or until filling is puffed and knife inserted into center comes out clean. Let stand 10 minutes before serving.

CARMEL CHICKEN FRESCO BAKE

Makes 8 servings

- **4 cups broccoli florets**
- **4 tablespoons butter, divided**
- **12 ounces cremini mushrooms, sliced**
- **3 shallots, diced**
- **1 can (14 ounces) artichoke hearts, drained and quartered**
- **¼ cup all-purpose flour**
- **2½ cups chicken broth**
- **1 teaspoon Dijon mustard**
- **½ teaspoon salt**
- **½ teaspoon dried tarragon**
- **½ teaspoon black pepper**
- **1 cup (4 ounces) shredded Emmentaler or Swiss cheese**
- **2 pounds boneless skinless chicken breasts, cooked and cut into 1½-inch cubes***
- **¼ cup grated Asiago cheese**

Or buy a rotisserie chicken and cut or shred the meat into 1½-inch pieces to equal 2 pounds.

1. Preheat oven to 350°F. Spray 4-quart baking dish with nonstick cooking spray.
2. Bring large saucepan of water to a boil. Add broccoli; cook 4 minutes. Rinse and drain under cold water to cool. Place in large bowl.
3. Melt 1 tablespoon butter in medium skillet over medium heat. Add mushrooms and shallots; cook and stir about 5 minutes or until softened. Add to bowl with broccoli. Stir in artichokes.
4. Melt remaining 3 tablespoons butter in same skillet. Stir in flour until blended. Add broth, mustard, salt, tarragon and pepper; whisk about 2 minutes or until sauce thickens. Add Emmentaler cheese; stir until smooth. Alternately layer chicken and vegetable mixture in prepared baking dish; pour cheese sauce over top.
5. Cover with foil and bake 40 minutes. Uncover; sprinkle with Asiago cheese. Bake 5 to 10 minutes or until cheese is melted.

MEXICAN LASAGNA

Makes 4 servings

- 1 pound ground beef
- 1 package (1½ ounces) taco seasoning mix
- 1 can (about 14 ounces) Mexican-style diced tomatoes
- 1½ teaspoons chili powder
- 1 teaspoon ground cumin
- ½ teaspoon salt
- ½ teaspoon red pepper flakes
- 2 cups (16 ounces) sour cream
- 1 can (4 ounces) diced mild green chiles, drained
- 6 green onions, chopped
- 6 to 7 medium (8-inch) flour tortillas
- 1 can (15 ounces) corn, drained
- 2 cups (8 ounces) shredded Cheddar cheese

1. Preheat oven to 350°F. Spray 13×9-inch baking dish with nonstick cooking spray.
2. Brown beef in large skillet over medium heat 6 to 8 minutes, stirring to break up meat. Drain fat; stir taco seasoning into beef.
3. Combine tomatoes, chili powder, cumin, salt and red pepper flakes in medium bowl. Combine sour cream, chiles and green onions in small bowl.
4. Layer one third of tomato mixture, two tortillas, one third of sour cream mixture, one third of beef mixture, one third of corn and one third of cheese in prepared baking dish. Repeat layers twice.
5. Bake 35 minutes or until bubbly. Let stand 15 minutes before serving.

LAMB & POTATO HOT POT

Makes 4 to 6 servings

- **3 tablespoons canola oil, divided**
- **1½ pounds boneless leg of lamb, cut into 1-inch cubes**
- **4 medium onions, thinly sliced**
- **3 carrots, thinly sliced**
- **1 teaspoon chopped fresh thyme**
- **2 tablespoons all-purpose flour**
- **1¼ cups chicken broth**
- **¾ teaspoon salt, divided**
- **¼ teaspoon black pepper**
- **3 medium russet potatoes (12 ounces), peeled and thinly sliced**
- **1 tablespoon butter, cut into small pieces**

1. Preheat oven to 350°F. Spray 2-quart baking dish with nonstick cooking spray.
2. Heat 2 tablespoons oil in large saucepan over medium-high heat. Add half of lamb; cook 4 to 5 minutes or until browned, turning occasionally. Remove to plate; repeat with remaining lamb.
3. Heat remaining 1 tablespoon oil in saucepan over medium-high heat. Add onions, carrots and thyme; cook 10 to 12 minutes or until onions are golden, stirring occasionally. Stir in lamb and any accumulated juices; cook 1 minute. Add flour; cook and stir 1 minute. Stir in broth, ½ teaspoon salt and pepper; bring to a boil and cook about 1 minute or until mixture starts to thicken. Transfer to prepared baking dish.
4. Arrange potato slices in overlapping layer over lamb mixture, starting from sides of casserole and working in towards center. Sprinkle potatoes with remaining ¼ teaspoon salt; dot with butter. Cover tightly with foil.
5. Bake 1 hour. Uncover; bake 15 to 20 minutes or until edges of potatoes are beginning to brown and lamb is tender.

TEX-MEX PASTA & TURKEY BAKE

Makes 6 servings

- **8 ounces uncooked mostaccioli or penne pasta**
- **2 teaspoons vegetable oil**
- **1 pound ground turkey**
- **1 package (10 ounces) frozen corn, thawed and drained**
- **⅔ cup salsa**
- **1 container (16 ounces) cottage cheese**
- **1 egg**
- **1 tablespoon minced fresh cilantro**
- **½ teaspoon white pepper**
- **¼ teaspoon ground cumin**
- **1 cup (4 ounces) shredded Monterey Jack cheese**

1. Preheat oven to 350°F. Spray 2-quart baking dish with nonstick cooking spray.
2. Cook pasta in large saucepan of salted boiling water according to package directions until al dente. Drain and set aside.
3. Heat oil in large nonstick skillet over medium-high heat. Add turkey; cook 6 to 8 minutes or until no longer pink, stirring to break up meat. Stir in corn and salsa. Remove from heat.
4. Combine cottage cheese, egg, cilantro, white pepper and cumin in small bowl. Spoon half of turkey mixture into prepared baking dish. Top with pasta. Spoon cottage cheese mixture over pasta. Top with remaining turkey mixture and sprinkle with Monterey Jack cheese.
5. Bake 25 to 30 minutes or until heated through.

STEAK & MUSHROOM PIE

Makes 4 to 6 servings

- 3 tablespoons butter, divided
- 1½ pounds boneless beef chuck steak, cut into 1-inch cubes
- 2 medium onions, chopped
- 3 stalks celery, cut into ½-inch slices
- 1 package (8 ounces) sliced mushrooms
- ½ teaspoon dried thyme
- ½ cup dry red wine
- ¼ cup all-purpose flour
- 1 cup beef broth
- 2 tablespoons tomato paste
- 1 tablespoon Dijon mustard
- ½ teaspoon salt
- ¼ teaspoon black pepper
- 1 refrigerated pie crust (half of 15-ounce package)
- 1 egg, lightly beaten

1. Spray 9- or 10-inch deep-dish pie plate or 1½-quart baking dish with nonstick cooking spray.

2. Melt 2 tablespoons butter in large saucepan over medium-high heat. Add half of beef; cook 4 to 5 minutes or until browned, turning occasionally. Remove to plate; repeat with remaining beef.

3. Melt remaining 1 tablespoon butter in same saucepan over medium-high heat. Add onions, celery, mushrooms and thyme; cook and stir 4 to 5 minutes or until vegetables begin to soften. Add wine; cook and stir 3 to 4 minutes or until almost evaporated. Add flour; cook and stir 1 minute. Stir in broth, tomato paste, mustard and beef; bring to a boil.

4. Reduce heat to medium-low; cover and simmer 1 hour to 1 hour 10 minutes or until beef is very tender, stirring occasionally. Remove from heat; stir in salt and pepper. Pour into prepared pie plate; let cool 20 minutes.

5. Preheat oven to 400°F. Roll out pie crust on lightly floured surface to fit top of pie plate. Place crust over filling; decoratively flute or crimp edges. Brush crust with egg; cut several small slits in top of crust with tip of knife.

6. Bake 23 to 25 minutes or until crust is golden brown. Let stand 5 minutes before serving.

SOUTHWEST TURKEY BAKE

Makes 8 servings

- 1 pound ground turkey
- 1 can (about 15 ounces) black beans, rinsed and drained
- 1 cup salsa
- ½ teaspoon ground cumin
- ⅛ teaspoon ground red pepper
- Salt and black pepper
- 1 package (8½ ounces) corn muffin mix
- ¾ cup chicken broth or milk
- 1 egg
- ¾ cup (3 ounces) shredded Mexican cheese blend
- Lime wedges (optional)

1. Preheat oven to 400°F.
2. Cook turkey in large nonstick skillet over medium-high heat 6 to 8 minutes or until no longer pink, stirring to break up meat. Stir in beans, salsa, cumin and red pepper; simmer 2 minutes. Season with salt and black pepper. Spoon turkey mixture into 13×9-inch baking dish.
3. Combine corn muffin mix, broth and egg in medium bowl; mix well. Spread over turkey mixture. Sprinkle evenly with cheese.
4. Bake 15 minutes or until edges are lightly browned. Serve with lime wedges, if desired.

PORK & CORN BREAD STUFFING CASSEROLE

Makes 4 servings

- ½ **teaspoon paprika**
- ¼ **teaspoon salt**
- ¼ **teaspoon garlic powder**
- ¼ **teaspoon black pepper**
- 4 **bone-in pork chops (about 1¾ pounds)**
- 2 **tablespoons butter**
- 1½ **cups chopped onions**
- ¾ **cup thinly sliced celery**
- ¾ **cup julienned or shredded carrots**
- ¼ **cup chopped fresh Italian parsley**
- 1 **can (about 14 ounces) chicken broth**
- 4 **cups corn bread stuffing mix**

1. Preheat oven to 350°F. Spray 13×9-inch baking dish with nonstick cooking spray.
2. Combine paprika, salt, garlic powder and pepper in small bowl; sprinkle over both sides of pork chops.
3. Melt butter in large skillet over medium-high heat. Add pork chops; cook about 4 minutes per side or just until browned. Remove to plate.
4. Add onions, celery, carrots and parsley to same skillet; cook and stir 4 minutes or until onions are translucent. Add broth; bring to a boil. Remove from heat; add stuffing mix and fluff with fork. Spoon into prepared baking dish; top with pork chops.
5. Cover and bake 25 minutes or until pork is barely pink in center.

Variation: For a one-dish meal, use an ovenproof skillet. Place the browned pork chops on the mixture in the skillet; cover and bake as directed.

TUNA PENNE CASSEROLE

Makes 6 servings

- **6 ounces penne pasta, uncooked**
- **1 can (10¾ ounces) condensed cream of chicken or celery soup, undiluted**
- **½ cup milk**
- **¼ cup mayonnaise**
- **½ teaspoon salt**
- **Pinch black pepper**
- **Pinch celery seed**
- **1 can (about 6 ounces) tuna, drained and flaked**
- **1 cup (4 ounces) shredded sharp Cheddar cheese**
- **½ cup sliced celery**
- **1 can (4 ounces) sliced water chestnuts, drained**
- **1 jar (2 ounces) chopped pimientos, drained**

1. Preheat oven to 350°F. Spray 2-quart baking dish with nonstick cooking spray.
2. Cook pasta in large saucepan of salted boiling water according to package directions for al dente. Drain and return to saucepan. Stir in soup, milk, mayonnaise, salt, pepper and celery seed; mix well. Gently stir in tuna, cheese, celery, water chestnuts and pimientos. Transfer to prepared baking dish.
3. Bake 25 minutes or until hot and bubbly.

HEARTLAND CHICKEN CASSEROLE

Makes 6 servings

- 10 slices white bread, cubed
- 1½ cups cracker crumbs or plain dry bread crumbs, divided
- 4 cups cubed cooked chicken
- 3 cups chicken broth
- 1 cup chopped onion
- 1 cup chopped celery
- 1 can (8 ounces) sliced mushrooms, drained
- 1 jar (about 4 ounces) pimientos, drained and diced
- 3 eggs, lightly beaten
- Salt and black pepper
- 1 tablespoon butter

1. Preheat oven to 350°F.
2. Combine bread cubes and 1 cup cracker crumbs in large bowl. Add chicken, broth, onion, celery, mushrooms, pimientos and eggs; mix well. Season with salt and pepper; spoon into 2½-quart baking dish.
3. Melt butter in small saucepan over low heat. Add remaining ½ cup cracker crumbs; cook and stir until golden. Sprinkle crumbs over casserole.
4. Bake 1 hour or until hot and bubbly.

MAIN MEATS

BBQ BABY BACK RIBS

Makes 4 servings

- **1¼ cups water**
- **1 cup white vinegar**
- **⅔ cup packed dark brown sugar**
- **½ cup tomato paste**
- **1 tablespoon yellow mustard**
- **1½ teaspoons salt**
- **1 teaspoon liquid smoke**
- **1 teaspoon onion powder**
- **½ teaspoon garlic powder**
- **½ teaspoon paprika**
- **2 racks pork baby back ribs (3½ to 4 pounds total)**

1. Combine water, vinegar, brown sugar, tomato paste, mustard, salt, liquid smoke, onion powder, garlic powder and paprika in medium saucepan; bring to a boil over medium heat. Reduce heat to medium-low; cook 40 minutes or until sauce thickens, stirring occasionally.
2. Preheat oven to 300°F. Place each rack of ribs on large sheet of heavy-duty foil. Brush some of sauce over ribs, covering completely. Fold down edges of foil tightly to seal and create packet; arrange packets on baking sheet, seam sides up.
3. Bake 2 hours. Prepare grill or preheat broiler. Carefully open packets and drain off excess liquid.
4. Brush ribs with sauce; grill or broil 5 minutes per side or until beginning to char, brushing with sauce once or twice during grilling. Cut into individual ribs; serve with remaining sauce.

TACOS WITH CARNITAS

Makes 8 servings

- 3 pounds pork shoulder or roast, trimmed of fat, cut into 3-inch pieces
- 1 medium onion, quartered
- 3 bay leaves
- 2 tablespoons chili powder
- 1 tablespoon plus ½ teaspoon salt, divided
- 1 tablespoon dried oregano
- 1 teaspoon ground cumin
- 1 cup chopped tomato
- 2 tablespoons minced onion
- 2 tablespoons minced fresh cilantro
- 2 tablespoons lime juice
- ½ jalapeño pepper, seeded and minced
- 1 clove garlic, minced
- 16 (6-inch) corn tortillas, warmed
- 4 cups shredded romaine lettuce
- Crumbled feta or cotija cheese
- 1 can (4 ounces) diced mild green chiles
- Optional toppings: pickled red onion, chopped fresh cilantro, diced avocado and/or lime wedges

1. Combine pork, onion, bay leaves, chili powder, 1 tablespoon salt, oregano and cumin in large saucepan or Dutch oven. Add enough water to cover pork. Cover; bring to a boil. Reduce heat to medium-low; simmer 3 hours or until pork is fork-tender.
2. Meanwhile for salsa, combine tomato, onion, 2 tablespoons cilantro, lime juice, jalapeño, garlic and remaining ½ teaspoon salt in small bowl; gently mix.
3. Preheat oven to 450°F. Transfer pork to large baking dish. Bake 20 minutes or until browned and crisp.
4. When cool enough to handle, shred pork with two forks. Add to saucepan; stir to coat. Cover and simmer 10 minutes or until most liquid is absorbed. Remove pork to medium bowl using slotted spoon; discard liquid.
5. Serve carnitas on tortillas with lettuce, cheese, green chiles, salsa and desired toppings.

RENEGADE STEAK

Makes 2 servings

- 1½ teaspoons coarse salt
- ½ teaspoon paprika
- ½ teaspoon black pepper
- ¼ teaspoon onion powder
- ¼ teaspoon garlic powder
- ⅛ teaspoon ground turmeric
- ⅛ teaspoon ground coriander
- ⅛ teaspoon ground red pepper
- 2 center-cut sirloin, strip or tri-tip steaks (about 8 ounces each)
- 2 tablespoons vegetable oil
- 1 tablespoon butter

1. Combine salt, paprika, black pepper, onion powder, garlic powder, turmeric, coriander and red pepper in small bowl; mix well. Season both sides of steaks with spice mixture (you will not need all of it); let steaks stand at room temperature 45 minutes before cooking.
2. Heat large cast iron skillet over high heat. Add oil; heat until oil shimmers and just begins to smoke. Add steaks to skillet; cook 30 seconds, then turn steaks. Cook 30 seconds, then turn again. Continue cooking and turning every 30 seconds for 4 minutes or until golden brown crust begins to form.
3. Add butter; continue cooking and turning every 30 seconds for 1 minute or until steaks reach 130° to 135°F for medium rare or 140° to 145°F for medium.* Remove to plate; let steaks rest 5 minutes before serving.

**Timing given is approximate for 1½-inch steaks; thinner steaks will take less time to cook.*

MEATLOAF

Makes 6 to 8 servings

- **1 tablespoon vegetable oil**
- **2 green onions, minced**
- **¼ cup minced green bell pepper**
- **¼ cup grated carrot**
- **3 cloves garlic, minced**
- **¾ cup milk**
- **2 eggs, beaten**
- **1 pound ground beef**
- **1 pound ground pork**
- **1 cup plain dry bread crumbs**
- **2 teaspoons salt**
- **½ teaspoon onion powder**
- **½ teaspoon black pepper**
- **½ cup ketchup, divided**

1. Preheat oven to 350°F.
2. Heat oil in large skillet over medium-high heat. Add green onions, bell pepper, carrot and garlic; cook and stir 5 minutes or until vegetables are softened.
3. Whisk milk and eggs in medium bowl until well blended. Gently mix beef, pork, bread crumbs, salt, onion powder and black pepper in large bowl with hands. Add milk mixture, vegetables and ¼ cup ketchup; mix gently. Press into 9×5-inch loaf pan; place pan on rimmed baking sheet.
4. Bake 30 minutes. Spread remaining ¼ cup ketchup over meatloaf; bake 1 hour or until cooked through (165°F). Cool in pan 10 minutes; cut into slices.

BAKED HAM WITH SWEET & SPICY GLAZE

Makes 8 to 10 servings

- **1 bone-in smoked half ham (8 pounds)**
- **¾ cup packed brown sugar**
- **⅓ cup cider vinegar**
- **¼ cup golden raisins**
- **1 can (8¾ ounces) sliced peaches in heavy syrup, drained, chopped and syrup reserved**
- **1 tablespoon cornstarch**
- **¼ cup orange juice**
- **1 can (8¼ ounces) crushed pineapple in syrup, undrained**
- **1 tablespoon grated orange peel**
- **1 clove garlic, minced**
- **½ teaspoon red pepper flakes**
- **½ teaspoon grated fresh ginger**

1. Preheat oven to 325°F. Place ham, fat side up, in roasting pan. Bake 3 hours.
2. For glaze, combine brown sugar, vinegar, raisins and peach syrup in medium saucepan. Bring to a boil over high heat. Reduce heat to low; simmer 8 to 10 minutes.
3. Whisk cornstarch into orange juice in small bowl until smooth and well blended. Stir into brown sugar mixture. Stir peaches, pineapple, orange peel, garlic, red pepper flakes and ginger into saucepan; bring to a boil over medium heat. Cook until sauce is thickened, stirring constantly.
4. Remove ham from oven. Generously brush half of glaze over ham; bake 30 minutes or until thermometer inserted into thickest part of ham registers 160°F.
5. Remove ham from oven; brush with remaining glaze. Let stand 20 minutes before slicing.

ROASTED CHICKEN & VEGETABLES

Makes 4 servings

- 1½ pounds russet potatoes or red potatoes, cut into wedges
- 2 large carrots, peeled and sliced diagonally
- 1 tablespoon olive oil
- 2½ teaspoons salt, divided
- 1 teaspoon black pepper, divided
- 1 whole chicken (about 4 pounds)
- 1 medium lemon
- 3 tablespoons butter, softened
- 2 cloves garlic, minced
- 1 teaspoon onion powder
- 1 teaspoon dried rosemary
- ½ teaspoon paprika
- 1 fresh rosemary or thyme sprig

1. Preheat oven to 425°F. Combine potatoes and carrots in 12-inch cast iron skillet or medium baking dish. Drizzle with oil and season with 1 teaspoon salt and ½ teaspoon pepper; toss to coat. Arrange around edge of skillet. Pat chicken dry; place on top of vegetables.
2. Juice lemon into small bowl; reserve squeezed lemon halves. Add butter, garlic, remaining 1½ teaspoons salt, onion powder, dried rosemary, paprika and remaining ½ teaspoon pepper to lemon juice; mash with fork until well blended. Loosen skin on breasts and thighs; spread about one third of butter mixture under skin.
3. Brush remaining butter mixture all over outside of chicken and inside cavity. Place one lemon half and rosemary sprig in cavity of chicken. Tie drumsticks together with kitchen string and tuck wing tips under.
4. Roast 20 minutes. *Reduce oven temperature to 375°F.* Roast 50 to 60 minutes or until chicken is cooked through (165°F) and vegetables are tender, basting once with pan juices during last 10 minutes of cooking time. Remove chicken to large cutting board; tent with foil. Let stand 15 minutes before carving.

TEXAS-STYLE BARBECUED BRISKET

Makes 10 to 12 servings

- 3 tablespoons Worcestershire sauce
- 2 cloves garlic, minced
- 1 tablespoon chili powder
- 1 teaspoon celery salt
- 1 teaspoon black pepper
- 1 teaspoon liquid smoke
- 1 beef brisket (3 to 4 pounds), trimmed
- 2 bay leaves

BARBECUE SAUCE

- 2 tablespoons vegetable oil
- 1 onion, chopped
- 2 cloves garlic, minced
- 1 cup ketchup
- ½ cup molasses
- ¼ cup cider vinegar
- 2 teaspoons chili powder
- ½ teaspoon dry mustard

SLOW COOKER DIRECTIONS

1. Combine Worcestershire sauce, garlic, chili powder, celery salt, pepper and liquid smoke in small bowl. Spread mixture on all sides of beef. Place beef in large resealable food storage bag; seal bag. Refrigerate 24 hours.
2. Place beef, marinade and bay leaves in slow cooker (cut meat in half to fit, if necessary). Cover; cook on LOW 7 hours.
3. Meanwhile for barbecue sauce, heat oil in medium saucepan over medium heat. Add onion and garlic; cook and stir until onion is tender. Stir in ketchup, molasses, vinegar, chili powder and dry mustard; simmer over medium heat 5 minutes.
4. Remove beef from slow cooker and pour juices into 2-cup measure; let stand 5 minutes. Skim fat from juices. Remove and discard bay leaves. Stir 1 cup juices into barbecue sauce. Discard remaining juices.
5. Return beef and sauce mixture to slow cooker. Cover; cook on LOW 1 hour or until meat is fork-tender. Remove beef to cutting board. Cut across grain into ¼-inch-thick slices. Serve with barbecue sauce.

SOUTHWESTERN LAMB CHOPS WITH CHARRED CORN RELISH

Makes 4 servings

LAMB

- 4 lamb shoulder or blade chops (about 8 ounces each), cut 1 inch thick and trimmed
- ¼ cup vegetable oil
- ¼ cup lime juice
- 1 tablespoon chili powder
- 2 cloves garlic, minced
- 1 teaspoon salt
- 1 teaspoon ground cumin
- ¼ teaspoon ground red pepper

CHARRED CORN RELISH

- 2 large ears fresh corn, husked and silk removed
- ½ cup diced red bell pepper
- ¼ cup chopped fresh cilantro

1. Place lamb in large resealable food storage bag. Combine oil, lime juice, chili powder, garlic, salt, cumin and red pepper in small bowl; mix well. Reserve 3 tablespoons mixture for corn relish; cover and refrigerate. Pour remaining mixture over lamb. Seal bag; turn to coat. Marinate in refrigerator at least 8 hours or overnight, turning occasionally.
2. Prepare grill for direct cooking. Grill corn, covered, over medium heat 10 to 12 minutes or until charred, turning occasionally. Let stand until cool enough to handle. Cut kernels off cobs into large bowl; scrape cobs with knife to release remaining corn and liquid. Add bell pepper, cilantro and reserved lime juice mixture to corn; mix well.
3. Remove lamb from marinade; discard marinade. Grill lamb, covered, over medium heat 13 to 15 minutes for medium (145°F) or to desired doneness, turning once. Serve with corn relish.

OVERSTUFFED MEXICAN-STYLE PEPPERS

Makes 4 servings

- 1 pound ground beef
- ½ cup finely chopped onion
- 1 can (about 4 ounces) chopped mild green chiles
- ½ cup corn
- ½ cup tomato sauce, divided
- ¼ cup cornmeal
- ½ teaspoon salt
- ½ teaspoon ground cumin
- 2 large green bell peppers, cut in half lengthwise, seeded and stemmed (about 8 ounces each)
- 1 cup (4 ounces) shredded sharp Cheddar cheese

1. Preheat oven to 375°F.
2. Cook beef and onion in large skillet over medium-high heat 6 to 8 minutes or until beef is browned and onion is softened, stirring to break up meat. Drain fat. Add chiles, corn, ¼ cup tomato sauce, cornmeal, salt and cumin; mix well.
3. Arrange pepper halves, cut side up, in 12×8-inch baking pan. Spoon beef mixture evenly into each pepper half. Spoon 1 tablespoon of remaining tomato sauce over beef mixture in each pepper.
4. Bake about 35 minutes or until peppers are tender. Sprinkle evenly with cheese. If desired, bake 5 minutes or until cheese is melted. Serve immediately.

ROASTED PORK TENDERLOIN WITH FRESH PLUM SALSA

Makes 4 servings

- 1 whole well-trimmed pork tenderloin (about 1 pound)
- ⅓ cup soy sauce
- 2 tablespoons plus 2 teaspoons lime juice, divided
- 1 tablespoon toasted sesame oil
- 2 cloves garlic, minced
- 2 cups coarsely chopped red plums (about 3)
- 2 tablespoons chopped green onion
- 4 tablespoons packed brown sugar, divided
- 1 tablespoon chopped fresh cilantro
- Dash ground red pepper

1. Place tenderloin in large resealable food storage bag. Combine soy sauce, 2 tablespoons lime juice, oil and garlic in small bowl. Pour over tenderloin. Seal bag tightly; turn to coat. Marinate in refrigerator overnight, turning occasionally.
2. For salsa, combine plums, green onion, 2 tablespoons brown sugar, cilantro, remaining 2 teaspoons lime juice and ground red pepper in medium bowl. Cover; refrigerate at least 2 hours.
3. Preheat oven to 375°F. Drain tenderloin, reserving 2 tablespoons marinade. Combine reserved marinade and remaining 2 tablespoons brown sugar in small saucepan. Bring to a boil over medium-high heat. Cook 1 minute, stirring once.
4. To ensure even cooking, tuck narrow end of tenderloin under roast, forming even thickness of meat. Secure with kitchen string. Place tenderloin on meat rack in shallow roasting pan. Brush with marinade mixture.
5. Bake 15 minutes; brush with remaining marinade mixture. Bake 5 to 10 minutes or until instant read thermometer registers 145°F when tested in thickest part of tenderloin.
6. Transfer tenderloin to cutting board; tent with foil. Let stand 10 minutes. Remove string from tenderloin; discard. Thinly slice tenderloin; serve with salsa.

SWEET & ZESTY SIRLOIN

Makes 4 servings

- ¼ **cup steak sauce**
- 2 **tablespoons ketchup**
- 1 **tablespoon sugar**
- 1 **tablespoon balsamic vinegar**
- 2 **teaspoons grated orange peel**
- ¼ **teaspoon salt**
- ¼ **teaspoon red pepper flakes**
- 1½ **pounds boneless sirloin steak, about ¾ inch thick**

1. Combine steak sauce, ketchup, sugar, vinegar, orange peel, salt and red pepper flakes in small bowl; stir until well blended.
2. Place steak on large plate. Reserve 3 tablespoons sauce mixture. Pour remaining sauce mixture over steak, turning several times to coat evenly. Marinate 10 minutes. Preheat broiler.
3. Coat broiler rack with nonstick cooking spray. Place steak on rack. Broil 5 minutes; turn. Broil 5 minutes more or until desired doneness.
4. Remove to cutting board; let stand 3 minutes. Slice diagonally and spoon reserved sauce over steak.

SIDE DISHES

SMASHED POTATOES

Makes 4 servings

- **4 medium russet potatoes (about 1½ pounds), peeled and cut into ¼-inch cubes**
- **⅓ cup milk**
- **2 tablespoons sour cream**
- **1 tablespoon minced onion**
- **½ teaspoon salt**
- **¼ teaspoon black pepper**
- **⅛ teaspoon garlic powder (optional)**
- **Chopped fresh chives or French fried onions (optional)**

1. Bring large saucepan of salted water to a boil over medium-high heat. Add potatoes; cook 15 to 20 minutes or until fork-tender. Drain and return to saucepan.

2. Slightly mash potatoes. Stir in milk, sour cream, minced onion, salt, pepper and garlic powder, if desired. Mash until desired texture is reached, leaving potatoes chunky. Cook 5 minutes over low heat or until heated through, stirring occasionally. Top with chives, if desired.

HUSH PUPPIES

Makes about 24 hush puppies

- 1½ cups yellow cornmeal
- ½ cup all-purpose flour
- 2 teaspoons baking powder
- ¾ teaspoon salt
- 1 cup milk
- 1 small onion, minced
- 1 egg, lightly beaten
- Vegetable oil

1. Combine cornmeal, flour, baking powder and salt in medium bowl; mix well. Add milk, onion and egg; stir until well blended. Let batter stand 5 to 10 minutes.
2. Heat 1 inch of oil in large heavy skillet over medium heat to 375°F; adjust heat to maintain temperature. Working in batches, drop batter by tablespoonfuls into hot oil; cook 2 minutes or until golden brown. Drain on paper towel-lined plate. Serve warm.

FRIJOLES BORRACHOS (DRUNKEN BEANS)

Makes 8 servings

- **6 slices bacon, chopped**
- **1 medium yellow onion, chopped**
- **1 tablespoon minced garlic**
- **3 jalapeño peppers, seeded and finely chopped**
- **1 tablespoon dried oregano**
- **1 bottle or can (12 ounces) beer**
- **6 cups water**
- **1 pound dried pinto beans, rinsed and sorted**
- **1 can (about 14 ounces) diced tomatoes**
- **1 tablespoon kosher salt**
- **¼ cup chopped fresh cilantro**

SLOW COOKER DIRECTIONS

1. Heat large skillet over medium-high heat. Add bacon; cook and stir 5 minutes or until mostly browned and crisp. Remove with slotted spoon to slow cooker. Discard all but 3 tablespoons drippings.
2. Heat same skillet over medium heat. Add onion; cook and stir 6 minutes or until softened and lightly browned. Add garlic, jalapeños and oregano; cook 30 seconds or until fragrant. Increase heat to medium-high. Add beer; bring to a simmer. Cook 2 minutes, stirring and scraping up any brown bits from bottom of skillet. Pour mixture into slow cooker. Stir in water, beans, tomatoes and salt.
3. Cover; cook on LOW 8 hours or on HIGH 6 hours or until beans are tender. Mash beans slightly until broth is thickened and creamy. Stir in cilantro.

CINNAMON APPLES

Makes 4 servings

- ¼ cup (½ stick) butter
- 3 tart red apples such as Gala, Fuji or Honeycrisp (about 1½ pounds total), peeled and cut into ½-inch wedges
- ¼ cup packed brown sugar
- 1 teaspoon ground cinnamon
- ⅛ teaspoon ground nutmeg
- ⅛ teaspoon salt
- 1 tablespoon cornstarch

1. Melt butter in large skillet over medium-high heat. Add apples; cook 8 minutes or until tender, stirring occasionally.
2. Add brown sugar, cinnamon, nutmeg and salt; cook and stir 1 minute or until apples are glazed. Reduce heat to medium-low; stir in cornstarch until well blended.
3. Remove from heat; let stand 5 minutes for glaze to thicken. Stir again; serve immediately.

GREEN BEANS WITH GARLIC-CILANTRO BUTTER

Makes 4 to 6 servings

- 1½ pounds green beans, trimmed
- 3 tablespoons butter
- 1 red bell pepper, cut into thin strips
- ½ sweet onion, halved and thinly sliced
- 2 teaspoons minced garlic
- 1 teaspoon salt
- 2 tablespoons chopped fresh cilantro
- Black pepper

1. Bring large saucepan of salted water to a boil over medium-high heat. Add beans; cook 5 minutes or until tender. Drain beans.

2. Meanwhile, melt butter in large skillet over medium-high heat. Add bell pepper and onion; cook and stir 3 minutes or until vegetables are softened but not browned. Add garlic; cook and stir 30 seconds. Add beans and salt; cook and stir 2 minutes. Stir in cilantro; season with black pepper. Serve immediately.

HEARTY HASH BROWN CASSEROLE

Makes about 16 servings

- **2 cups sour cream**
- **2 cups (8 ounces) shredded Colby cheese, divided**
- **1 can (10¾ ounces) cream of celery or chicken soup**
- **½ cup (1 stick) butter, melted**
- **1 small onion, finely chopped**
- **¾ teaspoon salt**
- **½ teaspoon black pepper**
- **1 package (30 ounces) frozen shredded hash brown potatoes, thawed**

1. Preheat oven to 375°F. Spray 13×9-inch baking dish with nonstick cooking spray.
2. Combine sour cream, 1½ cups cheese, soup, butter, onion, salt and pepper in large bowl; mix well. Add potatoes; stir until well blended. Spread mixture in prepared baking dish. (Do not pack down.) Sprinkle with remaining ½ cup cheese.
3. Bake 45 minutes or until cheese is melted and top of casserole is beginning to brown.

FRIED GREEN TOMATOES

Makes 4 servings

- **⅓ cup all-purpose flour**
- **½ teaspoon salt**
- **2 eggs**
- **1 tablespoon water**
- **½ cup panko bread crumbs**
- **2 large green tomatoes, cut into ½-inch-thick slices**
- **½ cup olive oil**
- **½ cup ranch dressing**
- **1 tablespoon sriracha sauce**
- **1 package (5 ounces) spring greens salad mix**
- **¼ cup crumbled goat cheese**

1. Combine flour and salt in shallow bowl. Beat eggs and water in another shallow bowl. Place panko in third shallow bowl. Coat both sides of tomato slices with flour mixture, shaking off excess. Dip in egg mixture, letting excess drip back into bowl. Roll in panko to coat. Place on plate.
2. Heat oil in large skillet over medium-high heat. Add half of tomato slices, arranging in single layer in skillet. (Cook in two or three batches as necessary; do not overlap in skillet.) Cook about 2 minutes per side or until golden brown. Remove to paper towel-lined plate.
3. Combine ranch dressing and sriracha in small bowl; mix well. Divide greens among four serving plates; top with tomatoes. Drizzle with dressing mixture; sprinkle with cheese.

LOADED BAKED POTATOES

Makes 4 servings

- 4 large baking potatoes
- 1 cup (4 ounces) shredded Cheddar cheese
- 1 cup (4 ounces) shredded Monterey Jack cheese
- 8 slices bacon, crisp-cooked
- ½ cup sour cream
- ¼ cup (½ stick) butter, melted
- 2 tablespoons milk
- 1 teaspoon salt
- ¼ teaspoon black pepper
- 1 tablespoon vegetable oil
- 2 teaspoons coarse salt
- 1 green onion, thinly sliced (optional)

1. Preheat oven to 400°F. Prick potatoes all over with fork; place in small baking pan. Bake 1 hour or until potatoes are fork-tender. Let stand until cool enough to handle. *Reduce oven temperature to 350°F.*
2. Combine Cheddar and Monterey Jack cheeses in small bowl; reserve ¼ cup for garnish. Chop bacon; reserve ¼ cup for garnish.
3. Cut off thin slice from one long side of each potato. Scoop out centers of potatoes, leaving ¼-inch shell. Place flesh from 3 potatoes in medium bowl. (Reserve flesh from fourth potato for another use.) Add sour cream, butter, remaining 1¾ cups shredded cheese, bacon, milk, 1 teaspoon salt and pepper to bowl with potatoes; mash until well blended.
4. Turn potato shells over; brush bottoms and sides with oil. Sprinkle evenly with coarse salt. Turn right side up and return to baking pan. Fill shells with mashed potato mixture, mounding over tops of shells. Sprinkle with reserved cheese and bacon.
5. Bake 20 minutes or until filling is hot and cheese is melted. Garnish with green onion.

CREAMY MACARONI & CHEESE

Makes 6 to 8 servings

- 1 package (16 ounces) uncooked ditalini pasta
- 6 tablespoons (¾ stick) butter, divided
- ¼ cup all-purpose flour
- 4 cups whole milk
- 1 teaspoon salt
- ¼ teaspoon ground nutmeg
- 8 ounces smoked mozzarella, shredded
- 5 ounces fontina cheese, shredded
- 5 ounces Asiago cheese, shredded
- 4 ounces Cheddar cheese, shredded
- ½ cup grated Romano cheese
- 1 clove garlic, minced
- ¼ teaspoon Italian seasoning
- 2 cups cubed French bread (½-inch cubes)

1. Preheat oven to 375°F. Cook pasta in large saucepan of salted boiling water 9 minutes or until al dente. Drain and set aside.
2. Melt 4 tablespoons butter in large saucepan over medium heat. Add flour; whisk until smooth and well blended. Slowly whisk in milk in thin, steady stream; add salt and nutmeg. Cook 7 minutes or until thickened, whisking frequently.
3. Combine mozzarella, fontina, Asiago and Cheddar cheeses in large bowl; reserve 1½ cups for topping. Gradually add remaining cheese mixture by handfuls to milk mixture, stirring until smooth after each addition. Stir in Romano cheese until blended. Add pasta; stir until well blended. Spread in 2-quart baking dish or individual baking dishes; top with reserved cheese mixture.
4. Melt remaining 2 tablespoons butter in large skillet over medium-high heat. Add garlic and Italian seasoning; cook and stir 30 seconds or until garlic is fragrant but not browned. Add bread cubes; stir to coat. Spread over top of pasta.
5. Bake 20 minutes or until cheese is bubbly and bread cubes are golden brown.

CREAMED SPINACH

Makes 4 servings

- 1 pound baby spinach
- ½ cup (1 stick) butter
- 2 tablespoons finely chopped onion
- ¼ cup all-purpose flour
- 2 cups whole milk
- 1 bay leaf
- ½ teaspoon salt
- Pinch ground nutmeg
- Pinch ground red pepper
- Black pepper

1. Bring medium saucepan of water to a boil over high heat. Add spinach; cook 1 minute. Drain and remove to bowl of ice water to stop cooking. Squeeze spinach dry; coarsely chop. Wipe out saucepan with paper towel.

2. Melt butter in same saucepan over medium heat. Add onion; cook and stir 2 minutes or until softened. Add flour; cook and stir 2 to 3 minutes or until slightly golden. Slowly add milk in thin, steady stream, whisking constantly until mixture boils and begins to thicken. Stir in bay leaf, ½ teaspoon salt, nutmeg and red pepper. Reduce heat to low; cook and stir 5 minutes. Remove and discard bay leaf.

3. Stir in spinach; cook 5 minutes, stirring frequently. Season with additional salt and black pepper.

MH
CLOSED
FOR
THE SEASON

SNACKS AND DRINKS

GUACAMOLE BITES

Makes 24 bites

- **2 tablespoons vegetable oil**
- **1¼ teaspoons salt, divided**
- **½ teaspoon garlic powder**
- **12 (6-inch) corn tortillas**
- **2 small ripe avocados**
- **2 tablespoons finely chopped onion**
- **1 tablespoon chopped fresh cilantro**
- **2 teaspoons lime juice**
- **1 teaspoon finely chopped jalapeño pepper *or* ¼ teaspoon hot pepper sauce**

1. Preheat oven to 375°F. Whisk oil, ¾ teaspoon salt and garlic powder in small bowl until well blended.
2. Use 3-inch biscuit cutter to cut out two circles from each tortilla to create 24 circles total. Wrap stack of tortilla circles loosely in waxed paper; microwave on HIGH 10 to 15 seconds or just until softened. Brush one side of each tortilla very lightly with oil mixture; press into 24 mini (1¾-inch) muffin cups, oiled side up. (Do not spray muffin cups with nonstick cooking spray.)
3. Bake about 8 minutes or until crisp. Remove to wire racks to cool.
4. Meanwhile for guacamole, cut avocados into halves and remove pits. Scoop pulp into large bowl; mash roughly, leaving avocado slightly chunky. Stir in onion, cilantro, lime juice, remaining ½ teaspoon salt and jalapeño; mix well.
5. Fill each tortilla cup with 2 to 3 teaspoons guacamole.

Tip: Use the leftover tortilla trimmings to make a crispy topping for soups, chilis and salads. Cut the tortillas into strips or bite-size pieces. Add enough vegetable oil to cover bottom of a skillet and heat until oil is hot (test by adding a piece of tortilla; the oil is hot enough when it forms bubbles around the edges). Cook tortilla pieces in batches until golden and crisp, stirring occasionally; drain on paper towels. Season with salt.

BUFFALO WINGS

Makes 4 servings

- **1 cup hot pepper sauce**
- **⅓ cup vegetable oil, plus additional for frying**
- **1 teaspoon sugar**
- **½ teaspoon ground red pepper**
- **½ teaspoon garlic powder**
- **½ teaspoon Worcestershire sauce**
- **⅛ teaspoon black pepper**
- **1 pound chicken wings, tips discarded, separated at joints**
- **Blue cheese or ranch dressing**
- **Celery sticks**

1. Combine hot pepper sauce, ⅓ cup oil, sugar, red pepper, garlic powder, Worcestershire sauce and black pepper in small saucepan; cook over medium heat 20 minutes. Pour sauce into large bowl.
2. Heat 3 inches of oil in large saucepan over medium-high heat to 350°F; adjust heat to maintain temperature during cooking. Add wings; cook 10 minutes or until crispy. Drain on wire rack set over paper towels.
3. Transfer wings to bowl of sauce; toss to coat. Serve with blue cheese dressing and celery sticks.

SPINACH-ARTICHOKE DIP

Makes 6 to 8 servings

- 1 package (8 ounces) baby spinach
- 1 package (8 ounces) cream cheese, softened
- ¼ cup mayonnaise
- 1 clove garlic, minced
- 1 teaspoon dried basil
- ½ teaspoon dried thyme
- ¼ teaspoon salt
- ¼ teaspoon red pepper flakes
- ¼ teaspoon black pepper
- 1 can (about 14 ounces) artichoke hearts, drained and chopped
- ¾ cup grated Parmesan cheese, divided
- Toasted French bread slices or tortilla chips

1. Preheat oven to 350°F. Spray 8-inch oval, round or square baking dish with nonstick cooking spray.
2. Place spinach in large microwavable bowl; cover and microwave on HIGH 2 minutes or until wilted. Uncover; let stand until cool enough to handle. Squeeze dry and coarsely chop.
3. Whisk cream cheese, mayonnaise, garlic, basil, thyme, salt, red pepper flakes and black pepper in medium bowl until well blended. Stir in spinach, artichokes and ½ cup Parmesan cheese. Spread in prepared baking dish; sprinkle with remaining ¼ cup Parmesan cheese.
4. Bake about 30 minutes or until edges are golden brown. Cool slightly; serve warm with toasted bread slices.

FRIED MACARONI & CHEESE BITES

Makes 48 pieces (about 8 servings)

- 8 ounces uncooked elbow macaroni
- 2 tablespoons butter
- 2 tablespoons all-purpose flour
- 2 cups milk
- 1 teaspoon salt, divided
- 2 cups (8 ounces) shredded Cheddar cheese
- 1 cup (4 ounces) shredded Swiss cheese
- 1 cup (4 ounces) shredded smoked Gouda cheese
- Vegetable oil for frying
- 3 eggs
- ¼ cup water
- 2 cups plain dry bread crumbs
- 1 teaspoon Italian seasoning
- Marinara sauce, heated

1. Cook macaroni in large saucepan of salted boiling water 7 minutes or until al dente. Drain and set aside.
2. Melt butter in same saucepan over medium-high heat. Whisk in flour until smooth; cook 1 minute, whisking frequently. Whisk in milk in thin, steady stream; cook about 8 minutes or until thickened, stirring frequently. Add ½ teaspoon salt. Gradually stir in cheeses until melted and smooth. Stir in macaroni.
3. Spray 9-inch square baking pan with nonstick cooking spray. Spread macaroni and cheese in prepared pan; smooth top. Cover with plastic wrap; refrigerate 4 hours or until firm and cold.
4. Turn out macaroni and cheese onto cutting board; cut into 48 pieces. Heat ½ inch of oil in large deep skillet or saucepan to 350°F over medium-high heat.
5. Whisk eggs and ¼ cup water in medium bowl. Combine bread crumbs, Italian seasoning and remaining ½ teaspoon salt in another medium bowl. Working with a few pieces at a time, dip macaroni and cheese pieces in egg, then toss in bread crumb mixture to coat. Place on large baking sheet. Dip coated pieces in egg mixture again; toss in bread crumb mixture to coat.
6. Fry in batches about 3 minutes or until dark golden brown, turning once, adjusting heat to maintain temperature during cooking. Remove to paper towel-lined wire rack. Serve warm with marinara sauce for dipping.

ONION RINGS

Makes about 20 onion rings

- 1 cup all-purpose flour, divided
- ½ cup cornmeal
- 1 teaspoon black pepper
- ½ teaspoon salt, plus additional for seasoning
- ¼ to ½ teaspoon ground red pepper
- 1 cup light-colored beer
- Rémoulade Sauce (recipe follows) or ranch dressing
- Vegetable oil for frying
- 6 tablespoons cornstarch, divided
- 2 large sweet onions, cut into ½-inch rings and separated

1. Combine ½ cup flour, cornmeal, black pepper, ½ teaspoon salt and red pepper in large bowl; mix well. Whisk in beer until well blended. Let batter stand 1 hour.
2. Prepare Rémoulade Sauce; refrigerate until ready to serve.
3. Heat 2 inches of oil in large saucepan or Dutch oven over medium-high heat to 360° to 370°F, adjusting heat to maintain temperature during cooking. Line large wire rack with paper towels.
4. Whisk 4 tablespoons cornstarch into batter. Combine remaining ½ cup flour and 2 tablespoons cornstarch in medium bowl. Thoroughly coat onions with flour mixture.
5. Working with one at a time, dip onion rings into batter to coat completely; carefully place in hot oil. Cook about four onion rings at a time 3 minutes or until golden brown, turning once. Remove to prepared wire rack; season with additional salt. Serve immediately with Rémoulade Sauce.

Rémoulade Sauce: Combine 1 cup mayonnaise, 2 tablespoons coarse-grain mustard, 1 tablespoon lemon juice, 1 tablespoon sweet relish, 1 teaspoon horseradish sauce, 1 teaspoon Worcestershire sauce and ¼ teaspoon hot pepper sauce in medium bowl; mix well.

WHITE SPINACH QUESO

Makes 4 to 6 servings

- **1 tablespoon olive oil**
- **1 clove garlic, minced**
- **1 tablespoon all-purpose flour**
- **1 can (12 ounces) evaporated milk**
- **½ teaspoon salt**
- **2 cups (8 ounces) shredded Monterey Jack cheese, divided**
- **1 package (10 ounces) frozen chopped spinach, thawed and squeezed dry**
- **Optional toppings: pico de gallo, guacamole, chopped fresh cilantro and queso fresco**
- **Tortilla chips**

1. Preheat broiler.
2. Heat oil in medium saucepan over medium-low heat. Add garlic; cook and stir 1 minute without browning. Add flour; whisk until smooth. Add evaporated milk in thin, steady stream, whisking constantly; stir in salt. Cook about 4 minutes or until slightly thickened, whisking frequently. Add 1½ cups Monterey Jack cheese; whisk until smooth. Stir in spinach. Pour into medium cast iron skillet; sprinkle with remaining ½ cup Monterey Jack cheese.
3. Broil 1 minute or until cheese is melted and browned in spots. Top with pico de gallo, guacamole, cilantro and queso fresco. Serve immediately with tortilla chips.

CHIPOTLE CHICKEN QUESADILLAS

Makes 5 servings (4 wedges each)

- **1 package (8 ounces) cream cheese, softened**
- **1 cup (4 ounces) shredded Mexican cheese blend**
- **1 tablespoon minced canned chipotle pepper in adobo sauce**
- **5 (10-inch) flour tortillas**
- **5 cups shredded cooked chicken (about 1¼ pounds)**

Optional toppings: guacamole, sour cream, salsa and chopped fresh cilantro

1. Combine cream cheese, Mexican cheese blend and chipotle pepper in large bowl; mix well.
2. Spread ⅓ cup cheese mixture over half of one tortilla. Top with about 1 cup chicken. Fold tortilla over filling and press gently. Repeat with remaining tortillas, cheese mixture and chicken.
3. Heat large nonstick skillet over medium-high heat. Spray outside of each quesadilla with nonstick cooking spray; cook quesadillas 2 to 3 minutes per side or until lightly browned.
4. Cut each quesadilla into four wedges. Serve with desired toppings.

WHITE SANGRIA

Makes 8 to 10 (10-ounce) servings

- **2 oranges, cut into ¼-inch slices**
- **2 lemons, cut into ¼-inch slices**
- **½ cup sugar**
- **2 bottles (750 ml each) dry, fruity white wine (such as Pinot Grigio), chilled**
- **½ cup peach schnapps**
- **3 ripe peaches, pits removed and cut into wedges**
- **2 cups ice cubes (about 16 cubes)**

1. Place orange and lemon slices in large punch bowl or pitcher. Pour sugar over fruit; mash lightly until sugar dissolves and fruit begins to break down.
2. Stir in wine, peach schnapps and peaches; mix well. Refrigerate at least 2 hours or up to 10 hours. Add ice cubes just before serving.

GINGER & APPLE SPRITZER

Makes 4 to 6 servings

- **3 English breakfast tea bags**
- **1 cup boiling water**
- **¼ cup sugar**
- **2 tablespoons minced crystallized ginger, plus additional for garnish**
- **2 tablespoons lemon juice**
- **3 cups sparkling apple cider, well chilled**
- **Ice**
- **Lemon wedges (optional)**

1. Place tea bags in 2-cup liquid measure. Add boiling water; steep tea 5 minutes. Remove and discard tea bags. Stir in sugar until dissolved. Refrigerate until cold.
2. Combine tea, 2 tablespoons ginger and lemon juice in tall pitcher. Stir well. (This can be done in advance and kept chilled for several hours.) Just before serving, pour in sparkling apple cider and stir gently to mix.
3. Pour into 4 to 6 ice-filled glasses. Spoon a little of the additional minced ginger into each glass. Garnish with lemon wedges.

GRAPEFRUIT-MINT ICED WHITE TEA

Makes 4 servings

- **4 cups hot brewed white tea**
- **½ cup sugar**
- **2 teaspoons chopped fresh mint**
- **1 cup fresh grapefruit juice**
- **1 cup ice cubes**

1. Combine hot tea, sugar and mint in large liquid measuring cup or medium pitcher; cool 10 minutes. Stir in juice.
2. Divide ice among glasses. Pour tea over ice.

Tip: If plain white tea is unavailable, try a tropical flavored tea instead.

WARM & SPICY FRUIT PUNCH

Makes about 14 (6-ounce) servings

- 4 cinnamon sticks
- Juice and peel of 1 orange
- 1 teaspoon whole allspice
- ½ teaspoon whole cloves
- 7 cups water
- 1 can (12 ounces) frozen cranberry-raspberry juice concentrate, thawed
- 1 can (6 ounces) frozen lemonade concentrate, thawed
- 2 cans (5½ ounces each) apricot nectar

SLOW COOKER DIRECTIONS

1. Break cinnamon sticks into pieces. Tie cinnamon sticks, orange peel, allspice and cloves in cheesecloth bag.
2. Combine orange juice, water, juice concentrates and apricot nectar in 4-quart slow cooker; add spice bag. Cover; cook on LOW 5 to 6 hours.
3. Remove and discard spice bag.

Note: If you don't have a cheesecloth bag, float the spices and orange peel in the juice and scoop them out with a small fine-mesh strainer.

STRAWBERRY LEMONADE

Makes 4 to 6 servings

- **3 cups water, divided**
- **1 cup sugar**
- **1 cup frozen strawberries**
- **1½ cups lemon juice**

1. Combine 1 cup water, sugar and strawberries in small saucepan; bring to a boil over high heat. Boil 5 minutes. Remove from heat; cool completely.
2. Pour strawberry mixture into blender; blend until smooth. Strain into pitcher. Stir in lemon juice and remaining 2 cups water until blended. Refrigerate until cold.

CHERRY LIMEADE

Makes 1 serving (about 12 ounces)

- **Crushed ice**
- **¼ lime**
- **1 can (12 ounces) lemon-lime soda**
- **2 tablespoons thawed frozen limeade concentrate**
- **2 tablespoons liquid from maraschino cherry jar**
- **1 maraschino cherry (optional)**

1. Fill tall glass with crushed ice. Squeeze lime wedge over ice and drop in lime.
2. Pour soda, limeade and cherry liquid into glass; stir gently. Garnish with maraschino cherry.

Tip: To make a fun and festive party drink for a crowd, combine two 2-liter bottles of chilled lemon-lime soda, two cans (12 ounces each) frozen limeade concentrate and two jars (10 ounces each) maraschino cherries (both juice and cherries) in a punch bowl or beverage dispenser.

CAKES, PIES AND MORE

WARM APPLE CROSTATA

Makes 4 tarts (4 to 8 servings)

- **1¾ cups all-purpose flour**
- **⅓ cup granulated sugar**
- **½ teaspoon plus ⅛ teaspoon salt, divided**
- **¾ cup (1½ sticks) cold butter, cut into small pieces**
- **3 tablespoons ice water**
- **2 teaspoons vanilla**
- **2 pounds Pink Lady or Honeycrisp apples, peeled and cut into ¼-inch slices**
- **¼ cup packed brown sugar**
- **1 tablespoon lemon juice**
- **1 teaspoon ground cinnamon**
- **⅛ teaspoon ground nutmeg**
- **4 teaspoons butter, cut into very small pieces**
- **1 egg, beaten**
- **1 to 2 teaspoons coarse sugar**
- **Vanilla ice cream**
- **Caramel sauce or ice cream topping**

1. Combine flour, granulated sugar and ½ teaspoon salt in food processor; process 5 seconds. Add ¾ cup cold butter; process 10 seconds or until mixture resembles coarse crumbs.

2. Combine ice water and vanilla in small bowl. With motor running, pour mixture through feed tube; process 12 seconds or until dough begins to come together. Shape dough into a disc; wrap with plastic wrap and refrigerate 30 minutes.

3. Meanwhile, combine apples, brown sugar, lemon juice, cinnamon, nutmeg and remaining ⅛ teaspoon salt in large bowl; toss to coat. Preheat oven to 400°F.

4. Line two large baking sheets with parchment paper. Cut dough into four pieces; roll out each piece into 7-inch circle on floured surface. Place on prepared baking sheets; mound apples in center of dough circles (about 1 cup apples for each crostata). Fold or roll up edges of dough towards center to create rim of crostata. Dot apples with 4 teaspoons butter. Brush dough with egg; sprinkle dough and apples with coarse sugar.

5. Bake 20 minutes or until apples are tender and crust is golden brown. Serve warm topped with ice cream and caramel sauce.

CHOCOLATE BUTTERMILK CAKE

Makes 12 servings

- **2 cups all-purpose flour**
- **3¼ cups sugar, divided**
- **⅔ cup unsweetened cocoa powder**
- **2 teaspoons baking soda**
- **1½ teaspoons baking powder**
- **¾ teaspoon salt**
- **1¾ cups buttermilk**
- **½ cup vegetable oil**
- **2 eggs**
- **2 teaspoons vanilla, divided**
- **6 ounces unsweetened chocolate, chopped**
- **½ cup (1 stick) butter, cut into small pieces**
- **1 cup whipping cream**

1. Preheat oven to 350°F. Line bottoms of two 9-inch cake pans with parchment paper; spray pans and paper with nonstick cooking spray.
2. Combine flour, 1¾ cups sugar, cocoa, baking soda, baking powder and salt in large bowl. Whisk buttermilk, oil, eggs and 1 teaspoon vanilla in medium bowl until well blended. Stir into flour mixture until well blended. Divide batter between prepared pans.
3. Bake 22 to 24 minutes or until toothpick inserted into centers comes out clean. Cool in pans 10 minutes. Remove to wire racks; cool completely.
4. Combine chocolate and butter in medium bowl. Heat remaining 1½ cups sugar and cream in small saucepan over medium-high heat, stirring until sugar is dissolved. When cream begins to bubble, reduce heat and simmer 5 minutes. Pour over chocolate and butter; stir until smooth. Stir in remaining 1 teaspoon vanilla. Refrigerate until frosting is cool and thickened, stirring occasionally.
5. Place one cake layer on serving plate; spread with 1 cup frosting. Top with second cake layer; frost top and side of cake with remaining frosting. Refrigerate at least 1 hour before slicing. Refrigerate leftovers.

PINEAPPLE UPSIDE DOWN CAKE

Makes 10 servings

TOPPING

- 1 small pineapple
- ¼ cup (½ stick) butter
- ½ cup packed brown sugar
- Stemmed maraschino cherries

CAKE

- 2 cups all-purpose flour
- 2 teaspoons baking powder
- ½ teaspoon baking soda
- ½ teaspoon salt
- ½ cup (1 stick) butter, softened
- 1 cup granulated sugar
- 1 egg
- 1 teaspoon vanilla
- 1 cup buttermilk

1. Preheat oven to 350°F. Spray 9-inch round baking pan with nonstick cooking spray. Remove top and bottom of pineapple. Cut off outside of pineapple and remove eyes. Cut pineapple crosswise into ¼-inch slices. Remove core with ½-inch cookie cutter or sharp knife.
2. For topping, cook and stir ¼ cup butter and brown sugar in medium skillet over medium heat until melted and smooth. Remove from heat. Pour into prepared pan. Arrange pineapple slices in pan, placing cherries in centers of pineapple and between slices. Reserve remaining pineapple for another use.
3. For cake, whisk flour, baking powder, baking soda and salt in medium bowl. Beat ½ cup butter and granulated sugar in large bowl with electric mixer on medium speed until well blended. Beat in egg and vanilla. Add flour mixture alternately with buttermilk, beating just until blended after each addition. Pour batter over pineapple.
4. Bake about 1 hour or until toothpick inserted into center comes out clean. Cool in pan on wire rack 10 minutes. Run thin knife around edge of pan to loosen cake. Invert onto serving plate. Cool completely.

Note: The cake can also be baked in a 10-inch cast iron skillet. Melt the butter and brown sugar in the skillet, add the pineapple and cherries and pour the batter over the fruit. Check the cake for doneness at 40 minutes.

CARROT CAKE

Makes 8 to 10 servings

CAKE

- 2 cups all-purpose flour
- 2 teaspoons baking soda
- 2 teaspoons ground cinnamon
- 1 teaspoon salt
- 4 eggs
- 2¼ cups granulated sugar
- 1 cup vegetable oil
- 1 cup buttermilk
- 1 tablespoon vanilla
- 3 cups shredded carrots
- 3 cups walnuts, chopped and toasted (see Note), divided
- 1 cup shredded coconut
- 1 can (8 ounces) crushed pineapple

FROSTING

- 2 packages (8 ounces each) cream cheese, softened
- 1 cup (2 sticks) butter, softened
- Pinch salt
- 3 cups powdered sugar
- 1 tablespoon orange juice
- 2 teaspoons grated orange peel
- 1 teaspoon vanilla

1. Preheat oven to 350°F. Spray two 9-inch round cake pans with nonstick cooking spray. Line bottoms with parchment paper; spray paper with cooking spray.
2. For cake, whisk flour, baking soda, cinnamon and 1 teaspoon salt in medium bowl. Whisk eggs in large bowl until blended. Add granulated sugar, oil, buttermilk and 1 tablespoon vanilla; whisk until well blended. Add flour mixture; stir until well blended. Add carrots, 1 cup walnuts, coconut and pineapple; stir just until blended. Pour batter into prepared pans.
3. Bake 25 to 30 minutes or until toothpick inserted into centers comes out clean. Cool in pans 10 minutes; remove to wire racks to cool completely.
4. For frosting, beat cream cheese, butter and pinch of salt in large bowl with electric mixer at medium speed 3 minutes or until creamy. Add powdered sugar, orange juice, orange peel and 1 teaspoon vanilla; beat at low speed until blended. Beat at medium speed 2 minutes or until frosting is smooth.
5. Place one cake layer on serving plate; spread with 2 cups frosting. Top with second cake layer; frost top and side of cake with remaining frosting. Press 1¾ cups walnuts onto side of cake. Sprinkle remaining ¼ cup walnuts over top of cake.

Note: To toast walnuts, spread on ungreased baking sheet. Bake in preheated 350°F oven 6 to 8 minutes or until lightly browned, stirring frequently.

TOFFEE CAKE WITH WHISKEY SAUCE

Makes 9 servings

- **8 ounces chopped dates**
- **2¼ teaspoons baking soda, divided**
- **1½ cups boiling water**
- **2 cups all-purpose flour**
- **½ teaspoon salt**
- **¾ cup (1½ sticks) butter, softened**
- **½ cup granulated sugar**
- **½ cup packed dark brown sugar**
- **2 eggs**
- **1 teaspoon vanilla**
- **1½ cups butterscotch sauce**
- **2 tablespoons whiskey**
- **1 cup glazed pecans* or chopped toasted pecans**
- **Vanilla ice cream**

Glazed or candied pecans may be found in the produce section of the supermarket with other salad toppings, or they may be found in the snack aisle.

1. Preheat oven to 350°F. Spray 9-inch square baking pan with nonstick cooking spray.
2. Combine dates and 1½ teaspoons baking soda in medium bowl. Stir in boiling water; let stand 10 minutes to soften. Mash with fork or process in food processor until mixture forms paste.
3. Whisk flour, remaining ¾ teaspoon baking soda and salt in medium bowl. Beat butter, granulated sugar and brown sugar in large bowl with electric mixer at medium speed 3 minutes or until creamy. Add eggs, one at a time, beating until well blended after each addition. Beat in vanilla. Add flour mixture alternately with date mixture at low speed, beating just until blended after each addition. Spread batter in prepared pan.
4. Bake about 30 minutes or until toothpick inserted into center comes out with moist crumbs. Cool in pan on wire rack 15 minutes.
5. Pour butterscotch sauce into medium microwavable bowl; microwave on HIGH 30 seconds or until warm. Stir in whiskey. Drizzle sauce over each serving; sprinkle with pecans and top with ice cream.

BERRY COBBLER WITH CHILI-SPICED CORN BREAD

Makes 6 to 8 servings

FILLING

- 2 cups thawed frozen cranberries
- 2 cups fresh blueberries
- 2 cups fresh raspberries
- 1 cup sugar
- 3 tablespoons cornstarch
- 1 tablespoon grated orange peel

CORNMEAL TOPPING

- ¾ cup cornmeal
- ½ cup all-purpose flour
- 2 tablespoons sugar
- 2 teaspoons ancho chili powder*
- ¾ teaspoon baking powder
- ¼ teaspoon baking soda
- ¼ teaspoon salt
- ¾ cup buttermilk, at room temperature
- 1 egg
- 2 tablespoons butter, melted

**If ancho chili powder is unavailable, substitute regular chili powder.*

1. Preheat oven to 400°F. Spray 8-inch square baking dish with nonstick cooking spray.
2. Combine cranberries, blueberries, raspberries, 1 cup sugar, cornstarch and orange peel in medium bowl; toss to coat. Spoon into prepared baking dish.
3. Combine cornmeal, flour, 2 tablespoons sugar, chili powder, baking powder, baking soda and salt in medium bowl; mix well. Stir in buttermilk, egg and melted butter just until moistened. Pour batter over fruit mixture, spreading evenly and leaving small border (about ½ inch) around edges of baking dish.
4. Bake about 35 minutes or until filling is thick and bubbly and corn bread topping is golden brown. Let stand 30 minutes before serving.

RHUBARB TART

Makes 8 servings

- **1 refrigerated pie crust (half of 15-ounce package)**
- **4 cups sliced fresh rhubarb (½-inch pieces)**
- **1¼ cups sugar**
- **¼ cup all-purpose flour**
- **2 tablespoons butter, cut into small pieces**
- **¼ cup old-fashioned oats**

1. Preheat oven to 450°F. Line 9-inch pie plate with crust; flute edge as desired.
2. Combine rhubarb, sugar and flour in medium bowl; toss to coat. Pour into pie crust. Dot with butter; sprinkle with oats.
3. Bake 10 minutes. *Reduce oven temperature to 350°F.* Bake 40 minutes or until filling is bubbly and crust is golden brown.

APPLE-PEAR PRALINE PIE

Makes 8 servings

- **Double-Crust Pie Pastry (recipe follows)**
- **4 cups sliced peeled Granny Smith apples**
- **2 cups sliced peeled pears**
- **¾ cup granulated sugar**
- **¼ cup plus 1 tablespoon all-purpose flour, divided**
- **4 teaspoons ground cinnamon**
- **¼ teaspoon salt**
- **½ cup (1 stick) plus 2 tablespoons butter, divided**
- **1 cup packed brown sugar**
- **1 tablespoon half-and-half or milk**
- **1 cup chopped pecans**

1. Prepare Double-Crust Pie Pastry.
2. Combine apples, pears, granulated sugar, ¼ cup flour, cinnamon and salt in large bowl; toss to coat. Let stand 15 minutes.
3. Preheat oven to 350°F. Roll out one disc of pastry into 11-inch circle on floured surface. Line deep-dish 9-inch pie plate with pastry; sprinkle with remaining 1 tablespoon flour. Spoon fruit mixture into crust.
4. Cut 2 tablespoons butter into small pieces. Scatter butter over fruit. Roll out remaining disc of pastry into 10-inch circle. Place over fruit; seal and flute edge. Cut slits in top crust.
5. Bake 1 hour. Place pie on wire rack.
6. For topping, combine remaining ½ cup butter, brown sugar and half-and-half in small saucepan; bring to a boil over medium heat, stirring frequently. Boil 2 minutes, stirring constantly. Remove from heat; stir in pecans. Spread over pie.
7. Cool pie on wire rack 15 minutes. Serve warm or at room temperature.

Double-Crust Pie Pastry: Combine 2½ cups all-purpose flour, 1 teaspoon granulated sugar and 1 teaspoon salt in large bowl. Cut in 1 cup (2 sticks) cold cubed unsalted butter with pastry blender or fingertips until coarse crumbs form. Combine 7 tablespoons ice water and 1 tablespoon cider vinegar in small bowl. Drizzle in just enough water mixture until dough starts to come together, stirring with fork. Turn out dough onto lightly floured surface; press into a ball. Divide in half. Shape each half into a disc; wrap in plastic wrap. Refrigerate at least 30 minutes.

CHOCOLATE CHIP COOKIE PIE

Makes 8 servings

- **1 refrigerated pie crust (half of 15-ounce package)**
- **¾ cup (1½ sticks) butter, softened**
- **½ cup granulated sugar**
- **½ cup packed brown sugar**
- **½ teaspoon vanilla**
- **¼ teaspoon salt**
- **2 eggs**
- **¾ cup all-purpose flour**
- **1 cup semisweet chocolate chunks or chips**
- **1 cup chopped nuts**
- **Flaky sea salt or coarse sugar (optional)**

1. Preheat oven to 325°F. Line 9-inch pie plate with crust; flute edge as desired.
2. Beat butter, granulated sugar, brown sugar, vanilla and salt in large bowl with electric mixer at medium speed until light and fluffy. Add eggs; beat until well blended. Beat in flour at low speed just until blended. Stir in chocolate chunks and nuts. Spread evenly in crust. Sprinkle with flaky salt or coarse sugar, if desired.
3. Bake 65 to 70 minutes or until toothpick inserted into center comes out clean. Cool completely on wire rack.

FARMHOUSE LEMON MERINGUE PIE

Makes 8 servings

- **1 unbaked frozen 9-inch frozen pie crust**
- **3 tablespoons lemon juice**
- **2 tablespoons butter, melted**
- **2 teaspoons grated lemon peel**
- **3 drops yellow food coloring (optional)**
- **⅔ cup sugar, divided**
- **1 cup cold water**
- **¼ cup cornstarch**
- **⅛ teaspoon salt**
- **4 eggs, at room temperature, separated**
- **¼ teaspoon vanilla**

1. Preheat oven to 425°F. Bake pie crust according to package directions.
2. Combine lemon juice, butter, lemon peel and food coloring, if desired, in small bowl; mix well.
3. Reserve 2 tablespoons sugar. Combine water, remaining sugar, cornstarch and salt in medium saucepan; whisk until smooth. Bring to a boil over medium-high heat, whisking constantly. Reduce heat to medium; boil 1 minute, whisking constantly. Remove from heat.
4. Stir ¼ cup hot sugar mixture into egg yolks in small bowl until well blended, whisking constantly. Slowly whisk egg yolk mixture back into hot sugar mixture. Cook over medium heat 3 minutes, whisking constantly. Remove from heat; stir in lemon juice mixture until well blended. Pour into baked pie crust.
5. Beat egg whites in large bowl with electric mixer at high speed until soft peaks form. Gradually beat in reserved 2 tablespoons sugar and vanilla; beat until stiff peaks form. Spread meringue over pie filling with rubber spatula, making sure meringue completely covers filling and touches edge of pie crust.
6. Bake 5 to 10 minutes or until meringue is lightly browned. Cool completely on wire rack. Lightly cover with plastic wrap; refrigerate 8 hours or overnight until filling is firm and pie is thoroughly chilled.

METRIC CONVERSION CHART

VOLUME MEASUREMENTS (dry)

1/8 teaspoon = 0.5 mL
1/4 teaspoon = 1 mL
1/2 teaspoon = 2 mL
3/4 teaspoon = 4 mL
1 teaspoon = 5 mL
1 tablespoon = 15 mL
2 tablespoons = 30 mL
1/4 cup = 60 mL
1/3 cup = 75 mL
1/2 cup = 125 mL
2/3 cup = 150 mL
3/4 cup = 175 mL
1 cup = 250 mL
2 cups = 1 pint = 500 mL
3 cups = 750 mL
4 cups = 1 quart = 1 L

VOLUME MEASUREMENTS (fluid)

1 fluid ounce (2 tablespoons) = 30 mL
4 fluid ounces (1/2 cup) = 125 mL
8 fluid ounces (1 cup) = 250 mL
12 fluid ounces (1 1/2 cups) = 375 mL
16 fluid ounces (2 cups) = 500 mL

WEIGHTS (mass)

1/2 ounce = 15 g
1 ounce = 30 g
3 ounces = 90 g
4 ounces = 120 g
8 ounces = 225 g
10 ounces = 285 g
12 ounces = 360 g
16 ounces = 1 pound = 450 g

DIMENSIONS

1/16 inch = 2 mm
1/8 inch = 3 mm
1/4 inch = 6 mm
1/2 inch = 1.5 cm
3/4 inch = 2 cm
1 inch = 2.5 cm

OVEN TEMPERATURES

250°F = 120°C
275°F = 140°C
300°F = 150°C
325°F = 160°C
350°F = 180°C
375°F = 190°C
400°F = 200°C
425°F = 220°C
450°F = 230°C

BAKING PAN SIZES

Utensil	Size in Inches/Quarts	Metric Volume	Size in Centimeters
Baking or Cake Pan (square or rectangular)	8×8×2	2 L	20×20×5
	9×9×2	2.5 L	23×23×5
	12×8×2	3 L	30×20×5
	13×9×2	3.5 L	33×23×5
Loaf Pan	8×4×3	1.5 L	20×10×7
	9×5×3	2 L	23×13×7
Round Layer Cake Pan	8×1½	1.2 L	20×4
	9×1½	1.5 L	23×4
Pie Plate	8×1¼	750 mL	20×3
	9×1¼	1 L	23×3
Baking Dish or Casserole	1 quart	1 L	—
	1½ quart	1.5 L	—
	2 quart	2 L	—